M000230070

SECRET HANDSHAKES
AND ROLLED-UP
TROUSER LEGS

THE SECRETS OF FREEMASONRY – FACT AND FICTION

SECRET HANDSHAKES AND ROLLED-UP TROUSER LEGS

THE SECRETS OF FREEMASONRY – FACT AND FICTION

RICHARD GAN

Lewis Masonic

First published 2014

ISBN 978 0 85318 441 6

All rights reserved. No part of this book may be reproduced or transmitted in any form or by any means, electronic or mechanical, including photocopying, recording or by any information storage and retrieval system, without permission from the Publisher in writing.

© Richard Gan, 2014

Richard Gan is hereby identified of the author of this work in accordance with Section 77 of the Copyright, Designs and Patents Act 1988.

Published by Lewis Masonic

an imprint of Ian Allan Publishing Ltd, Hersham, Surrey KT12 4RG.

Printed in England

Visit the Lewis Masonic website at www.lewismasonic.co.uk

Copyright
Illegal copying and selling of publications deprives authors, publishers and booksellers of income, without which there would be no investment in new publications. Unauthorised versions of publications are also likely to be inferior in quality and contain incorrect information. You can help by reporting copyright infringements and acts of piracy to the Publisher or the UK Copyright Service.

Cover image Steve Chadburn

Image Credits Authors' Lodge No. 3456, p.29; Chris Christodoulou – chris@photochris.co.uk, p.102, p.103; Globe Lodge No. 23, p.99; Paul Hurst, p.11; Burne James, p.48; Library and Museum of Freemasonry, p.30, p.34, p.35, p.50, p.58, p.70, p.81, p.89, p.108, p.112, p.122; Pioneer Lodge No. 9065, p.110; Powysland Museum, p.109; David Sharpe, p.32; South Wales Regalia – swregalia@aol.com, p.28; the Author, p.46, p.69, p.72, p.85, p.104, p.114.

Dedication

To my wife Niki
for her patience, encouragement
and support

Acknowledgements

I would like to record my thanks to Martin Cherry of the Library and Museum of Freemasonry, Ann Pilcher-Dayton and Pip Faulks for their help and assistance in the writing of this book.

Contents

Bibliography and Suggested Reading List   **127**

About the Author

Richard Gan is a senior Freemason and a Grand Officer in all the major Orders of Freemasonry. He retired in June 2010 as Deputy Grand Secretary of the Grand Lodge of Mark Master Masons, following which for four years he was the Editor of *The Square,* an independent magazine for Freemasons.

Born in 1950, he was educated at the Becket School, Nottingham, and is a graduate of London University where he took an Honours Degree in Geology and subsequently studied part-time for a Masters Degree in Education. He is also a graduate of the Open University, where he took a Bachelor of Arts Degree in Management Studies. Whilst at the Institute of Education he combined winning a double distinction in the Post Graduate Certificate of Education with serving as President of the Students' Union.

He has enjoyed a number of successful careers during his working life – as a teacher and head of faculty; a chief local government officer in educational administration; bursar and clerk to the governing body at a grant maintained school; Assistant Grand Secretary and subsequently Deputy Grand Secretary of the Grand Lodge of Mark Master Masons based in St James's; has held the equivalent post in the seven Masonic Orders administered from Mark Masons' Hall; and has been Editor of *The Square.* Having fully retired, he intends to make more time to extend his Masonic writing and research.

He lives near the border of Lincolnshire and Nottinghamshire with his wife Niki, who is a former preparatory school headmistress.

Richard Gan

Preface

The genesis of this book came about after I had spoken at a Rotary meeting about Freemasonry. It soon became apparent to me that the mixed audience, all of whom (bar two) were not Freemasons, had very many prejudices and very little knowledge about Freemasonry. The few things that most non-Masons are able to say about Freemasonry are that it is a secret society, whose members attend meetings where they wear aprons, roll-up their trouser legs and identify each other by secret handshakes – hence the title *Secret Handshakes and Rolled-Up Trouser Legs*. The main purpose of this book is to attempt to redress the balance, hence the sub-title *The Secrets of Freemasonry: Fact and Fiction*.

There have been books written in the past purporting to expose the secrets of Freemasonry. By and large these have been written by non-Masons and have generally been both negative and antagonistic towards Freemasons and Freemasonry, missing critical nuances and making unjustified assumptions. There have also been books written by Freemasons aimed primarily at new Freemasons, and as such these have tended to go over the heads of non-Masons.

This book is written with the non-Mason specifically in mind, by a senior Freemason and Grand Officer with over thirty years experience of the Craft. The concept behind it is to provide an opportunity for a non-Mason to find out what Freemasonry is all about. It does not set out in any way to proselytise, neither does it attempt to justify the case for the existence of Freemasonry. Indeed, having read the book, the reader may well still continue to be left feeling antagonistic towards Freemasonry but at least will be better informed as to the reasons why.

The majority of books written about Freemasonry start with some form of historical perspective in an attempt to put the subject matter into context. I have started by asking myself what is it that the reader actually wants to know? In the first instance it is not the historical background or the good works that might be done by the Freemasons, but rather the elements of secrecy, power, influence and corruption.

The one thing that most people seem to know about Freemasonry relates to the secret handshakes and raised trouser legs, both of which will be fully explained.

I have attempted to tackle the issues likely to be of most interest to the non-Masonic reader in as full a way as possible. The book is not intended to be an academic tome and so does not use footnotes or endnotes. There are, however, some issues that deserve to be covered in a little more depth. Hence, the format adopted in the second part of the book is encyclopaedic, laid out in alphabetical order. This will enable the reader to have the choice of reading the first part of the book from start to finish and then to dip in and out of the second part on an eclectic basis. Alternatively, the opportunity is there for looking up the relevant section in the second part of the book whilst reading the first part.

If you really want to know the truth behind all the myths and misconceptions about Freemasonry, this is the book for you!

Richard Gan
March 2014

Introduction

This book deals with some of the central themes in Freemasonry, which are outlined below. It will try to correct the misapprehensions and myths commonly found and give the non-Masonic reader a factual account of Freemasonry today.

What is Freemasonry?

Freemasonry is the oldest and largest initiatory, non-religious, fraternal organisation in this country dating back to, at least, the seventeenth century. A number of key principles have been in place since Freemasonry was first formally organised in the early eighteenth century and these include: a requirement to believe in the existence of God; a male-only membership; charitable giving and receiving; members to be of good morals.

Some basic facts about Freemasonry include the following:

Oldest

The historical origin of Freemasonry is even now far from clear. Theories that it can trace its origins back to ancient Egypt and links with the medieval Knights Templar make good and exciting fiction but not good history. The earliest English reference to somebody becoming a Freemason dates back to 1646. In Scotland there are slightly earlier references that link gentlemen becoming members of a lodge or company of working stonemasons. The term lodge is derived from the name of the temporary shelter put up at the side of the building and which housed the masons during its construction.

Largest

Freemasonry exists in some 164 countries with a total membership in the order of six million. Although by far the largest fraternal organisation in the world, the number of Freemasons worldwide is lower today than it has ever been. A fate shared by all types of membership organisations, ranging from Rotary, Scouts, Round Table, Knights of Columba, the Church, political parties, trade unions, golf clubs – the list is almost endless. At its peak in England there were some 500,000 members and in the USA over four million. Today there are about 300,000 Freemasons in England and in the USA some 1.3 million.

Initiatory

There are a considerable number of organisations who, as part of their joining procedure, require a candidate to go through some form of initiation ceremony. Freemasonry is by the far the best known but others include fraternal organisations such as: the Knights of Columba, fraternities and sororities in the USA, trade unions, the military, gangs, and certain tribal communities.

Non-religious

All Masonic meetings and ceremonies start and end with prayer – but then so do those of other organisations such as Parliament and local Councils. Freemasonry is not in any way a quasi-religion, nor a substitute for religion.

Fraternal organisation

A fraternity is more than just a social organisation. In a fraternity members freely associate as equals for a mutually beneficial purpose.

God

It is a prerequisite of membership that all candidates profess a belief in a Supreme Being – God. The term Supreme Being is used so as to be neither prescriptive nor exclusive of any particular religion or belief. When a lodge is in session a Volume of the Sacred Law is always open and displayed. 'Volume of the Sacred Law' is a synonym for the holy book of the various world religions including the Bible, *Bhagavad Gita*, *Granth Sahib*, *Koran*, and *Zenda Avesta*. In England the Volume of the Sacred Law would normally be the Bible. If the candidate is not of the Christian faith, then every effort is made to obtain and display the appropriate Volume.

Male membership

Freemasonry has been a solely male organisation ever since its formal organisation in England in 1717. Worldwide, there are separate Masonic and Co-Masonic organisations for women and men and women respectively. At the time of its establishment society was very much male-orientated so it is hardly surprising that Freemasonry originated as a male-only organisation.

Charitable Giving

From its inception Freemasonry has always been a major supporter of charities, both Masonic and non-Masonic. Since 1980 the Grand Charity (one of five major Masonic Charities), as well as providing for Freemasons and their dependents, has donated over £50 million to national charities in the form of grants. One essential difference between Masonic and other charities is that contributions are donated entirely from the membership rather than the public at large.

Charitable Receiving

The Committee of Charity was established in the early eighteenth century to help relieve the suffering of Masons and the dependants of deceased Masons with grants of up to five guineas each.

In 1788, Chevalier Bartholomew Ruspini and the Duchess of Cumberland founded a school for the daughters of distressed Masons, 'The Royal Cumberland Freemasons' School for Female Objects'. A similar provision for boys was established in 1798.

Good Morals

Freemasonry has a very low threshold for tolerating misdemeanours amongst its membership. In England any member convicted of a criminal offence resulting in a custodial or community sentence can expect to be expelled from the membership.

PART I

....

The Secrets of Freemasonry: Separating Fact and Fiction

The majority of books written about Freemasonry start with some form of historical perspective, in an attempt to put the subject matter into context. I have started by attempting to put myself in the place of a non-Masonic reader – what does he or she actually want to know about Freemasonry? I have come to the conclusion that what people really want to know about is the secret handshake and rolled-up trouser legs, rather than the historical background – what is of interest are the elements of supposed secrecy, power, influence and corruption rather than the charitable and good works that Freemasonry actually undertakes.

Part I of the book examines topics such as: What is a lodge? What really goes on in the Lodge Room? Where do Freemasons meet? Do they really wear aprons at lodge? How does one become a member? How much does it cost to be a Freemason? How do they get the best jobs? How do they always get their Planning Permissions through? How do they avoid getting caught by the Police? If they do go to Court, how do they manage to get off? So who are these Freemasons? Meeting on the Level.

What is a Lodge?

Freemasons or Masons – there is little practical difference between the two – meet in units called lodges. The lodge can refer to the unit itself or the meeting room in which the lodge takes place. All lodges have a name and a number: numbers have been allocated in sequential order, hence the lower the number the older the lodge. I have the privilege of belonging to Globe Lodge No. 23 which was constituted in 1723. The name Globe is derived from nothing more romantic than the name of the tavern in the Strand where the lodge used to meet early in its existence. It was fairly common for a lodge to be named after the tavern in which it met. These days there are very few restrictions in naming a lodge, save that it would be most unusual for a lodge to be named after a living person – a similarity incidentally shared in the naming of public houses. At the time of writing, the most recent lodge to be founded is City Gate Lodge No. 9890. In England there are some 8,000 lodges; the apparent discrepancy between the two figures is that, not surprisingly, over the last 300 years a number of lodges have ceased to exist, and numbers are not re-issued. A further complication is that on two occasions Grand Lodge has taken the opportunity of dealing with extinguished Lodges by removing them from the list and re-numbering those remaining. On the one hand Lodges were pleased because they were now allocated a lower number, but the Lodge Treasurer would have been far from pleased because it necessitated having new letterheads and summons engraved. The number of Freemasons in England is currently something in excess of 250,000.

Whilst Freemasonry exists worldwide in what used to be termed the 'free world', this book predominantly concerns itself with Freemasonry in England.

Freemasonry is and has been proscribed by extreme right and left wing governments at both ends of the political spectrum. Freemasonry was proscribed in Nazi Germany, in the Communist block in general and the USSR in particular. The notable exception was Cuba, were it has always operated quite freely. With the collapse of the Soviet Union, Freemasonry has re-emerged in Russia and the former states of the USSR. Not insignificantly, it is currently proscribed in Pakistan and a number of Islamic states but not (interestingly enough) in Malaysia, where it is flourishing.

To all intents and purposes, Masonic lodges are independent private clubs. To become a member, as with most clubs, one needs to be proposed and seconded by two existing members. The other members then vote whether to accept the man being put forward for membership. The vote is by secret ballot. If one has no objection to his proposed membership then a white ball is put in a bag (or specially designed ballot box) or a black ball if one does object – hence the expression '...to be blackballed'. Potential members are blackballed if one or sometimes two black balls appear in the ballot. The number of balls required depends on the individual rules of the lodge known as bylaws. In practice, the excitement of a genuine blackballing rarely occurs. Candidates are usually interviewed by a committee of senior members of the lodge and if there is likely to be any difficulty then the Proposer and Seconder are warned well in advance, and are given the opportunity of withdrawing their candidate's name before it goes to a formal ballot of the members.

If, for the moment, one thinks of the lodge as just another type of club, then it is not unreasonable to have a Chairman, elected by the members and holding office for one year. Save that in Masonry he is called the Master or more accurately the Worshipful Master. On more than one occasion, when having volunteered that I am a Freemason, and the person I am talking to takes a benign view of Freemasonry, something is said to the effect of 'oh, my grandfather (father or whatever) was a Mason, and was a Grand Master of his lodge.' Grand Master, very unlikely, but Worshipful Master almost certainly.

In the stratified world of Masonry, all Brethren are equal but some are more equal than others. Everybody initiated into Freemasonry starts as a Brother and indeed ends up as a Brother but when he becomes Master of his lodge he is then entitled to the appellation Worshipful and so is styled Worshipful Brother or W Bro.

Not only is Masonry stratified, it is also pyramidal in structure. At the base of the pyramid we have the lodges. The lodges in a particular area are grouped together as Provinces which, to a large extent, mirror the geographical counties and are termed Provincial Grand Lodges, of which there are forty-eight in England. Not to confuse matters, there are Provinces overseas, but these are called Districts, to distinguish them from those in England. A Provincial Grand Lodge is presided over by a Provincial Grand Master. As he is important, he is a Right Worshipful Brother; his deputy however is not as important and so is styled Very Worshipful Brother. At the top of the pyramid is Grand Lodge, ruled by the Grand Master, who is styled Most Worshipful Brother.

One of the reasons why it is unlikely that the man in our anecdote was probably not a Grand Master is quite simply that since 1967 the Grand Master in England has been HRH The Duke of Kent – and long may he continue.

Interestingly enough, the progression from Brother is mirrored in other organisations, not least the Church, where a priest starts as a Reverend, becomes an Archdeacon and a Very Reverend, progresses to Bishop as a Right Reverend and ultimately, when he becomes Archbishop of Canterbury, Most Reverend. Similar appellations are used when addressing the Mayor of a town – the Worshipful the Mayor or, in the case of a city, the Right Worshipful the Lord Mayor. Magistrates are referred to as Their Worships; and London Livery Companies are also called Worshipful – by way of example, the Worshipful Company of Wax Chandlers.

The likelihood of the average priest becoming a Right Reverend, let alone Most Reverend, is about as likely as the average Mason becoming a Right Worshipful.

Indeed, most Masons would give an arm or a leg just to become a Grand Officer, let alone a Very Worshipful, but more of that later. I include a disclaimer for those readers who take these things literally. Masons do not give an arm or a leg to become a Grand Officer, even though many might wish to do just that, were there such a scheme available. The same applies to the Obligation or oath taken by all Masons on their Initiation, where, to the best of my knowledge and belief, no Mason has ever had to submit to the traditional penalty of having his throat cut across for disclosing the secrets of Freemasonry.

Accepting the fact that a lodge is just a private club with a chairman known as the Worshipful Master – what then of the other officers of the lodge? As might reasonably be expected, as in any club or organisation, every lodge has a complement of regular officers who hold office for one or more years. These include a Secretary and a Treasurer, who effectively manage the day-to-day affairs of the lodge.

A lodge will also have an Almoner, who acts as the focal point for keeping in touch with members who are not enjoying the best of health or are perhaps in need of financial assistance, together with the widows of past members of the lodge. The latter may receive at worst a card and/or a present at Christmas, and at best financial assistance can be arranged if required. The Charity Steward of the lodge coordinates and encourages financial donations that are kept in a separate Charity or Benevolent Fund lodge account, to keep it separate and distinct from the General Lodge Account that is used for the day-to-day running of the lodge. Another key officer within the lodge is the Director of Ceremonies, or DC for short. The term Master of Ceremonies sums up his role: the key word is ceremonies. To understand the function of the DC and other officers, such as the Wardens, Deacons and Inner Guard, requires some explanation as to what goes on during a lodge meeting, but more of that later.

One very important distinction between Freemasons and other worthy organisations such as Rotary International, the Lions or Round Table is that all monies collected, whether ultimately used for Masonic or non-Masonic charities, comes from the pockets of the members and not the general public.

Much is made of the fact that Freemasons always look after their own – which is absolutely true – but not the whole story. At the time that Freemasonry was formally established in this country in 1717 there was no unemployment benefit, no national insurance scheme to provide pensions, no national health service and no one to bury you if you could not afford it. A number of organisations have been set up over the years to provide such services and give a financial safety net to its members. Examples include City Guilds and London Livery Companies, trade unions, Oddfellows and the like.

It is still true today that if a Freemason or one of his dependants falls on hard times there are a number of Masonic Charities that will be able to assist. These include the Freemasons' Grand Charity that provides assistance in the case of individual hardship. The Royal Masonic Trust for Girls and Boys aims to relieve poverty and advance the education of children of a Masonic family: to qualify for support a family must have suffered a distress which has resulted in financial hardship. The Royal Masonic Benevolent Institution has been caring for older Freemasons and their dependants for over 160 years and operates 17 residential care homes across England and Wales. The Masonic Samaritan Fund provides grants to those who have an identified health or care need and, faced with a long wait for treatment, care or support, are unable to afford their own private care.

All of which sounds terrific and of course it is, but it does not tell the full story. The advances in state provision, particularly since the Second World War, mean that many Freemasons and their dependants no longer need the level of care and assistance the various Masonic Charities previously provided. The criteria used to decide whether or not financial assistance can be given are very similar to those used by the state agencies. Very useful to catch those who fall through the net or whom for whatever reason the state is unable to help. It means that in recent years the various Masonic Charities have made and continue to make sizable grants to a vast range of non-Masonic charities. The purpose of this book is not to extol the virtues of Freemasonry as such and information about the range of work being done is easily found through the Internet. Suffice it to say that you would be very surprised at both the range and size of the grants being made. It certainly will not be found in any of the national newspapers, but more often than not may be found in the local press. I recall a grant of £3.1 million being made to the National Osteoporosis Society in 2006 to celebrate the sesquicentenary of a Masonic organisation – absolutely no mention in any of the national media, despite it being the largest grant ever received by the Society.

What goes on in the Lodge Room?

So what goes on at lodge meetings? In essence, a lodge night is composed of three elements: the meeting itself, pre-dinner drinks and dinner. A normal lodge meeting also consists of three parts: an opening ceremony, a degree ceremony and a closing ceremony, interspersed with items of administrative business. All in all, a lodge meeting would normally last some two hours. Pre-dinner drinks and dinner then follow. It is not unusual for the key members of a lodge to hold a rehearsal of the degree ceremony, either before the formal meeting starts or more likely in the week previous. Although practice varies, most lodge meetings take place in the evening, starting between 5.00 and 6.00 p.m. and finishing after dinner at about 10.00 p.m.

Craft Freemasonry consists of Three Degrees or ritual ceremonies. The word Craft is the generic term used for mainstream Freemasonry in this country. A new member is initiated into the First Degree (an Entered Apprentice), passed to the

Second Degree (a Fellowcraft) and raised to the Third Degree (a Master Mason). The number of times that a lodge meets during the course of a year varies considerably. The average is probably four or five, though some lodges do meet eleven or even twelve times a year. In some lodges a new member might be initiated at one meeting, passed at the next and raised at the one after that. In other words, he could become a fully-fledged Freemason – a Master Mason – in something less than a year. Other lodges take a more relaxed view and a candidate may find that he only takes one Degree each year and hence it takes him some three years to become a Master Mason. The timescale is entirely a matter for the individual lodge. The only other ceremony that a lodge will work is that of the Installation of the new Master together with the appointment of the various lodge officers for the ensuing year.

In order to ensure that the ceremony is carried out to best effect, many lodges hold a weekly Lodge of Instruction (LOI). The meeting is to all intents and purposes a simplified lodge meeting: the prime purpose being to rehearse the various Masonic ceremonies. After the LOI the members will often stay for a drink. The LOI may take place in the same building in which the lodge normally meets, but it would not be unusual for the LOI to take place in a private room in a local hostelry.

There has always been considerable public interest in and fascination with the various Masonic ceremonies. It is also true that right from the formal inception of Freemasonry in this country in 1717 the so-called secrets of Freemasonry have been the subject of what is known in Masonic circles as 'Exposures'. The earliest known Exposure dates back to 1723 and others have followed at regular intervals up to the present time!

If anyone is particularly interested, a copy of the ritual can be bought from any Masonic supplier or more easily obtained through the Internet – and you do not even have to give a password – some secret society! Whilst I am happy to relate and highlight certain aspects of the ritual ceremonies, there has to be a limit – for no better reason than a potential Freemason might be reading this book before deciding whether to proceed. In the same spirit as not wishing to spoil a film for somebody who has yet to see it by telling them the ending, I will refrain from giving all the details – besides which I would not wish to have my throat cut for doing so! (Just a joke).

To make sense of Masonic ceremonial it is important to appreciate that almost everything to do with Masonic ritual is surrounded with symbolism. A quick and simple example is that in every Lodge Room there will be found two small cubic stones, one roughly hewn with uneven surfaces, the other smooth with square corners – the rough and smooth ashlars – symbolically representing the increase in knowledge and wisdom of a Freemason, who arrives in the lodge as an ignorant Entered Apprentice and through the process of education has the 'corners knocked off' to become wiser, more knowledgeable and polished. Not exactly intellectually demanding stuff, but remember that the ritual dates back to the late eighteenth century and the ceremonies are one-act, allegorical plays.

The ritual or ceremonial of the Three Degrees in Freemasonry are progressive and follow a similar pattern. There is a different Opening/Closing procedure for each individual Degree, which ensures that those present are properly qualified to participate in that part of the ceremony. Then an introduction, where it is ascertained and made clear to those present that, whilst the Candidate is not yet a member of that particular Degree he has the necessary attributes and qualities to enable him to receive the appropriate secrets and become qualified. The blessing of God is invoked on the proceedings. An Obligation or oath is taken by the Candidate, in which he promises not to divulge the secrets that are about to be entrusted to him. Having taken the Obligation, the Candidate is entrusted with the secrets associated with the particular Degree. These usually consist of a sign, a grip or token of recognition and a secret word or series of words.

The sign is only given in a Lodge Room as part of a ceremony, as indeed are secret words associated with each Degree. In so far as the signs are concerned, they would look distinctly odd if given in a public place, rather than in a Lodge Room. The Pope giving the blessing *Urbe et Orbe* from the balcony in St Peter's Square on Easter Sunday gives some indication of the style. It would certainly be a give-away if a Mason entered a room and gave one of the three signs, hoping to attract the attention of or be recognised by a fellow Mason. This would surely invite notice and ensure that any other self-respecting Mason in the room would look away and/or make a rapid exit or both. There is a famous incident when in 1912 a man called Seddon, having been found guilty of murder, gave the sign of either the First Degree or Third Degree (eyewitness accounts vary) in an attempt to influence the judge to overturn the jury's decision. The judge, Sir Thomas Bucknill, who happened to be the Provincial Grand Master for Surrey, gave him very short shrift and is reported as saying with some emotion:

> It is not for me to harrow your feelings – try to make peace with your Maker. We both belong to the same Brotherhood, and though that can have no influence with me, this is painful beyond words to have to say what I am saying, but our Brotherhood does not encourage crime, it condemns it.

The secret word, or rather words as there are three, one for each of the three Degrees, are just that. As with the three signs, it is difficult to imagine a situation where a Mason goes up to someone and whispers in his ear one of the three secret words. In the lodge the secret word is used in a symbolic way, simply to confirm that those there are entitled to be present during that part of the ceremony. I have already alluded to Masonic 'Exposures'. Such was the interest in the eighteenth century in the secrets of Freemasonry that the words of the First and Second Degrees became well known in the public domain – so much so that in an effort to keep these secret Grand Lodge actually swopped the words over so that the original word in the First Degree became the one for the Second and vice versa. In 1813 the original designations were restored.

The grip or token of recognition is 'the secret handshake' of the title of the book. This token or handshake is supposed, in theory, to enable one Mason to recognise another by day as well as by night. The word 'supposed' is important. Whilst a limp handshake is usually a sure indication that the person concerned is not a Freemason, a firm handshake is no certainty that he is. Each of the three degrees requires pressure to be applied to a different part of the other's hand. Easier said than done. During the course of a lodge meeting great care is taken to ensure that the thumb is placed in exactly the right position, with clinical precision if the Director of Ceremonies has anything to do with it. Out of the Lodge Room it is not easy to reproduce with any degree of certainty. It may be difficult to believe, but it is extremely unlikely that a Freemason would recognise a fellow Freemason simply through the means of a handshake! Think about it next time you shake hands and you will see exactly what I mean. Not that long ago I was playing for my golf club and, as one does, was chatting to one of the opposition as we walked round. During the conversation it came out that I was a Freemason; my opponent told me that whilst he was not, he had discovered earlier in the same round that my partner was a Freemason! The sad truth for the conspiracy theorists is that although my playing partner and I had each been Freemasons for over thirty years, neither of us recognised the fact through a handshake.

I have previously likened the various Masonic ceremonies to one-act allegorical plays, that in many ways are not dissimilar to medieval Mystery Plays. When carried out well, the ceremonies would do credit to any amateur dramatic society. The majority of the ceremony is carried out by the Master of the Lodge and is done from memory. In some lodges, Past Masters will share part of the ceremony to help spread the workload. This book is not meant to be an exposé or indeed 'Exposure' of Masonic ritual. Nor is the ritual or ceremony of Initiation peculiar to Freemasonry. Other fraternal organisations such as the Knights of Columbus have similar ritual ceremonies, as did until comparatively recently various trade unions.

The title of the book refers to *Secret Handshakes* and *Rolled-Up Trouser Legs*. I am sure that I have disappointed readers with the 'exposé' on the former and I am afraid I must also do so with the latter.

A Candidate when he enters the Lodge Room for the first time is specially attired for the occasion. Shirt unbuttoned to expose his left breast; left trouser leg rolled up; and wearing a slipper on his right foot. Any metallic substances such as coins, watch and indeed cufflinks are left behind in the Preparation Room until after the ceremony.

This may all sound fairly ridiculous but, as indicated earlier, nearly everything to do with Masonic ritual is symbolic. Thus the Candidate enters the Room metaphorically poor and penniless. His right foot is slipshod; in Middle Eastern culture the removal of a shoe is an accepted method of entering into a solemn and legal agreement. The Candidate has to declare during the ceremony that he is a 'free man'. In the past slaves would be required to wear an ankle chain that would leave a permanent scar. Exposing the left leg demonstrates the lack of any such scar.

Although this whole scenario may appear absurd to the outside world – and I for one would not try to defend that observation – the fact of the matter is that every other person in that Lodge Room has undergone exactly the same ceremony. It serves several different purposes: to the Candidate a situation he is unlikely to forget, a reminder that he arrives at the door poor and penniless and suitably humbled. As far as the other members of the lodge are concerned, not only does it remind them of their own Initiation but it is also part of the bonding process. In so far as the ridicule is concerned the Masonic Initiation ceremony is no different in style to many other Initiation ceremonies found in the student world, the completion of apprenticeships, trade unions and other fraternal societies.

Freemasonry has been accused of many things over the years, including the fact that it is either a religion, a quasi-religion or even an alternative to religion. I do not pretend to be either a theologian or very much of a philosopher and if anyone is interested in exploring these issues any further there are a multiplicity of books on this particular aspect available on the market. For my part, the closest one gets to a religious element that takes place in the Lodge Room is the opening and closing prayers, and when the blessing of God is invoked on the proceedings during a ceremony. In some lodges it is the practice for an opening and closing ode to be sung.

Incidentally, all Masonic prayers end with the words *So mote it be* rather than *Amen*. The reason for this is that after the constitution of the United Grand Lodge of England in 1813, specifically Christian references were removed from the ritual – notwithstanding that at the time Christianity was the established religion of England. And so there is nothing whatsoever in any Craft Masonic ritual that any member of any religious belief would find either offensive or unacceptable. All lodges in this country have to have a copy of a Volume of the Sacred Law open during the meeting. The choice of words is not accidental. Whilst in the majority of cases the Volume will be the Bible, there is no reason why it should not be one of the holy books belonging to one of the major religions such as: the Koran, Torah, *Bhagavad Gita*, *Ramayana*, *Rig Veda*, and *Avesta*. If a Candidate for Freemasonry is not a Christian then most lodges will make every effort to ensure that he takes his Masonic Obligation on the holy book of his religion.

This brings us to two further issues that are of some concern to those outside Freemasonry. The first is the unequivocal requirement that all candidates for Freemasonry profess a belief in a Supreme Being. To all intents and purposes in this country it is a belief in God, but as indicated above other religions have different names and concepts of God; all of which are entirely acceptable as far as Freemasonry is concerned. What is not acceptable is atheism or non-belief.

The concept of starting a meeting with prayer is not unique to Freemasonry. In this country Parliament starts each daily sitting with prayers, as do most local authority Council meetings. What is clear is that whilst this concept has until very recently been accepted as part of the fabric of our society, it is now being increasingly challenged in the progressively secular society in which we live. Even the Scout and Guide Movements have in recent years been forced to adopt a secular oath for their members. The point here is that opening a lodge meeting with prayer does not constitute the meeting as a religious ceremony, any more than starting a session of Parliament does.

The other issue that perplexes many non-Masons is the blood-curdling Obligations that are taken by Candidates. Freemasons do not take an oath that is defined as 'a solemn appeal to a deity'. They take an Obligation that may be defined as 'something by which a person is bound or obliged to do as a sense of duty'. The latter is important, because as part of the ceremony the Candidate is told during the preamble before been asked to take his Obligation: '...*but let me assure you that in those vows there is nothing incompatible with your civil, moral, or religious duties.*' The best known of the Obligations is that associated with the Initiation into the First Degree as an Entered Apprentice, which apart from anything else involves – '*having your throat cut across should you improperly disclosed the secrets of Masonry*'. The Candidate is also advised that the penalty is traditional and that the '...*inclusion of such a penalty is unnecessary for the Obligation you have taken this evening is binding upon you for so long as you shall live...*'. To the best of my knowledge and belief, as they say in legal circles, no one in this country has ever suffered any of the penalties detailed in the various Obligations.

I say in this country, because there was an infamous allegation in the USA that one William Morgan was done away with by American Freemasons in 1826 for doing just that. Needless to say there is far more detail to the case and its aftermath than can be covered here, but suffice it to say that there is no definitive proof that, if anything untoward happened to Morgan, it was at the hands of the Freemasons. I have on previous occasions alluded to the historical context in which Freemasonry was first formalised and Masonic Obligations fall into that category. In other words, in the early eighteenth century the format and content of the Obligations would not have seemed at all extraordinary. Whilst it is clear that the penalties contained in the Obligations would never have been carried out, for the avoidance of any doubt, as early as 1979 the present Grand Master, HRH The Duke of Kent raised his concerns regarding the wording and in 1985 when presiding at Grand Lodge said: 'It seems to me that it would not be a very radical step, and would in no way affect the meaning of the Ritual, if the penalties were removed entirely from the Obligations, and treated as a form of traditional history.' Although it took a little time, by 1987 all references to physical penalties had been omitted from the Obligations taken by Candidates in the Three Degrees, but reference to the traditional penalties remained in other parts of the ceremonies so as to give meaning to the 'signs' of the Degrees. Whilst there is little doubt that 'The existence of the physical penalties... gives ready material for attack by our enemies and detractors', as the Board of General Purposes observed in its 'Report on the Penalties in the Obligations' in 1986, there is equally no doubt in my mind that the omission of the penalties will have made not one iota of difference to the enemies and detractors of Freemasonry.

This book is not in any way a defence of Freemasonry. If Freemasonry were to be founded today, it would be extremely different, as it would be a reflection of current society in the same way that it was a reflection of society in 1717. In many ways the language used in the ritual of Masonic ceremonies bears comparison to that in the Book of Common Prayer and indeed the King James' Bible. The Church of England has in recent times tried to adapt, to modernise its liturgy and the language used, with the introduction of the Alternative Service Book and new editions of the Bible. Notwithstanding the changes, it is true to say that many traditionalists still feel more comfortable with the Book of Common Prayer and the King James' Bible, in the same way that Freemasons feel comfortable with their own traditions. Rotary International, which in many ways is a similar organisation to Freemasonry, was founded as recently as 1905. Amongst other things it has an oath of allegiance and women were not allowed into full membership until the 1980s. The only point that I am trying to make is that an organisation is a product of the time of its formation. Some organisations adapt and evolve during the passage of time. Freemasonry in many respects has not and in that regard still reflects the mores, principles and high moral standards prevalent at the time of its formation. Freemasonry continues to instil in its members a moral and ethical approach to life: its values are based on integrity, kindness, honesty and fairness. Members are urged to regard the interests of the family as paramount but, importantly, Freemasonry also teaches concern for people, care for the less fortunate and help for those in need. Contrary to its public perception Freemasonry genuinely tries to make good men better.

Masonic aprons and collars as worn by a Grand Officer; Provincial Grand Officer; Worshipful Master; Master Mason; Fellow Craft and Entered Apprentice.

Do they really wear Aprons at Lodge?

Almost everything associated with Freemasonry is symbolic. Freemasonry as we know it today is believed to have developed from the original craft of stonemasonry – a transition that has taken place over a number of years from operative, or working stonemasonry, to speculative, or symbolic, Freemasonry.

Operative stonemasons traditionally wear long, leather aprons that are tied with a loop at the front, with the ends hanging loose. This is replicated in Freemasonry, albeit with a smaller apron, traditionally made of white lambskin, with a triangular flap. The type of apron worn designates the rank of the wearer.

On being initiated an Entered Apprentice wears a plain, white, lambskin apron; on being passed to the Second Degree he wears a white lambskin apron adorned with two blue rosettes; and on being raised to the Third Degree, three blue rosettes with the apron edged in light blue, moiré silk. On being installed as the Master of a Lodge the rosettes are replaced with silver levels.

The apron changes once Provincial rank is achieved, with the levels in gold, the apron edged in dark blue, moiré silk and the rank of the holder depicted in an embroidered roundel in the centre of the apron.

Appointment to Grand Rank results in the apron becoming more elaborate still, with the rank of the holder embroidered into the centre of the lambskin and considerable amounts of gold braid embroidery.

Once a Mason has been installed as a Master he is also entitled to wear a Past Master's Collar of light blue, moiré silk appended with a jewel depicting his rank – a square and compass. A Provincial or Grand Officer will wear a collar of dark blue, moiré silk with jewel appended to it denoting his rank.

The net result is that a Mason's rank and status within the organisation is evident and easily recognisable from the regalia that he wears in lodge.

In addition to an apron, the other item of regalia worn by all Freemasons is a pair of white gloves. The symbolism behind this is that everything a Freemason does should be pure and spotless and hence by wearing gloves it means that everything he touches will be with 'clean' hands.

There are other pieces of regalia, such as medals, that are also a regularly worn by Masons and these are known in Masonic circles as jewels. These jewels are usually issued to celebrate some form of Masonic anniversary. For example, once a

A Founder's Jewel and Past Master's Jewel belonging to Authors' Lodge No. 3456; Rudyard Kipling was an honorary member.

Master has completed his year in the Chair he is usually awarded a Past Master's breast jewel to wear in perpetuity. The form of the jewel varies but usually incorporates the lodge logo or motif. Jewels may also be struck to be worn to celebrate the founding of a lodge and, at the other end of the scale, to commemorate the centenary or even bicentenary of a lodge.

Freemasons like Masonic 'bling', and hence there is a ready market for such things as Masonic rings, tie-pins and cufflinks. Masonic ties are another popular area of Masonic wear. Nearly every Masonic Province has its own dedicated tie, as indeed does Grand Lodge. Designs vary considerably but will usually include some form of logo and, as often as not, the depiction of a square and compass.

Where do they meet?

The average number of members in a lodge is about thirty. The number varies up and down the country. In London it may be as low as twenty; in the provinces

Freemasons' Hall, the headquarters of the United Grand Lodge of England in Great Queen Street, London. A Grade II* listed building and one of the finest examples of Art Deco in the country. The building is open to the public and there are regular tours of both the Grand Temple and the Library and Museum of Freemasonry.

seventy or eighty members is not unusual. No two lodges are the same. They differ for a number of reasons, one of which is location. It is possible to group lodges into three very broad categories: those that meet in London; in large urban conurbations; and those that meet in small provincial towns and villages. London is in a unique situation not mirrored anywhere else in the world. There are some 1,400 lodges and 40,000 Freemasons meeting within five miles of the centre of London, a large number of them at Freemasons' Hall in Great Queen Street – the headquarters of English Freemasonry. The greater majority of those Freemasons will either work or have previously worked in London and live out in the suburbs. It means that the members of the lodge meet together but at the end of the evening disperse to all parts of the metropolis. The situation is mirrored in other cities such as Manchester, Liverpool and Nottingham, amongst many others.

One of the heydays of Masonry was the period immediately prior to the Second World War and it was at this time that a large number of purpose-built and imposing Masonic Halls were erected, including Freemasons' Hall in London, which in addition to the spectacular Grand Temple has twenty-one purpose-built lodge rooms. It is a Grade II* listed building, open to the public and it is one of the finest examples of Art Deco in the country. The Halls in the three cities mentioned above were also built at about the same time and boast similar facilities, albeit on a smaller scale.

In the suburbs lodges tend to meet in purpose-built or adapted centres. For example, in Middlesex there are five Masonic Centres. The one in Twickenham was previously a hotel and was converted for Masonic use back in the 1950s. Some one hundred different units meet there, which is approximately the same number as meet in the whole of Nottinghamshire. In so far as provincial towns and villages are concerned, not unexpectedly the number of lodges is very much smaller. By way of example, a town such as Newark-on-Trent, with a population of approximately 26,000, has one meeting place, a converted large suburban villa that is home to five lodges. Most of the members will live and work in the locality and even in a large town such as Newark may well come across each other in other aspects of community life.

A smaller town may well only have one lodge meeting there, either in its own premises or perhaps in a local hotel. A favourite conversion for a meeting place is that from a church or chapel. Given the internal height of such buildings, it is relatively easy to put in a new floor so that the Lodge Room can be accommodated on the first floor with the dining room on the ground floor, together with space for a bar and changing facilities. A small extension at the back is usually sufficient for the kitchen, and any garden left over makes a useful car park. A lodge based in a village or rural area may not have the resources or a suitable site for its own Masonic

The Masonic Hall, Loughborough is one example of the range of Masonic premises that are used for Masonic meetings throughout the country.

meeting place. It is not unusual for a village hall to be used for that purpose – the main room being used as the Lodge Room and after the meeting the Lodge Room is broken down by the members and converted into a dining room. Whilst this is being done the other members and visitors to the lodge can enjoy a few drinks – the number of drinks often being governed by the length of time it takes to convert the room from one use to the other! In such circumstances it is not unusual for the wives of the members to be responsible for preparing the food, which would then be served by the Stewards of the lodge. At the other end of the spectrum, lodges meeting in London are just as likely to dine somewhere like the Connaught Rooms, immediately next door to Freemasons' Hall, a nearby pub, restaurant or hotel or even one of the London Clubs; the ambience and the cost varying accordingly. In the provinces the meal following the meeting may cost in the order of £20.00 including wine, whilst in London the cost is likely to be in the order of £50.00, rising to £75.00 or more at a five-star hotel or restaurant in a London Club.

Most Masonic premises will have the square and compasses emblem displayed somewhere on the building, which is a bit of a give-away. These days it would not be unusual for the Masonic Hall to be called something like the…Suite or…Banqueting Rooms. This reflects the fact that most Masonic Halls need to supplement their income from sources other than Masonry, and are more than willing to hire the premises out for weddings, conferences and the like. Given that the criteria for an ideal Masonic premises is a large meeting space, dining room, bar, changing/cloakroom facilities, commercial kitchen and adequate parking, it also makes an excellent space for community use. Far from trying to be secretive, Masons are more than happy for their presence in the locality to be known.

I will say a little about the layout of a Lodge Room, for no other reason than that by not doing so I may be perceived as being guarded. The principal officers of the lodge have already been identified and during the course of a meeting will be seated in designated places around the Lodge Room. On entering a Lodge Room laid out for a meeting the most striking features are the squared, black and white carpet and the Master's Chair and pedestal in the 'east'. 'East', because in an ideal world it should be in the east, to mark the rising sun. In practice it is not always possible to have the Master in the East, hence back to the symbolic nature of Freemasonry. The black and white carpet is said to symbolise the light and darkness of everyday life – the ups and the downs. The three most senior officers of the lodge are the Master, who sits in the east, the Senior Warden in the west and the Junior Warden in the south. The Secretary and Treasurer sit at a table opposite the Junior Warden in the north. There are two Deacons: the Senior sits to the right of the Master and the Junior on the right of the Senior Warden. Their role is to act as 'messengers' for the Master and Senior Warden respectively during the various Masonic ceremonies. The Inner Guard, as far as practicable, sits on the left of the Senior Warden. One of his tasks is to announce the arrival of Brethren into the lodge and make sure that anybody not qualified is denied entry. The first of the 'progressive' officers in a lodge is the Steward. A lodge is likely to have more than one Steward at any one time. Although they do not play an active part in the Lodge Room they do afterwards at the dinner, or Festive Board as it is known in Freemasonry, where their main function is to serve the wine to all those present. Being appointed a Steward is the first step to eventually becoming Master of the Lodge. A process known as 'buggins-turn', the seniority of membership within a Lodge is governed by the date one joined. The reason the various 'floor' offices referred to previously are known as 'progressive' is quite simple. On the completion of his year as Master, one becomes (not that surprisingly) the Immediate Past Master, and as such one of the Past Masters of the lodge. In the ordinary course of events, the Senior Warden is elected Master and at the Installation ceremony after he is installed as Master he appoints in his place as Senior Warden the current Junior Warden, and then fills the subsequent vacancy caused. Thus everybody moves up a step: Steward moves to Inner Guard, who moves to Junior Deacon who moves to Senior Deacon who moves to Junior Warden – 'buggins-turn'! From first joining a lodge it can take anything from eight to thirteen years to reach the Chair as Master; occasionally it can be less, particularly if the Lodge is small in number or if other circumstance intervene, such as one of the 'progressive' officers having to drop out for some reason – redundancy, posting overseas, ill-health or whatever.

An explanation of the symbolism relating to the layout of the Lodge Room and the role played by all the various officers in the ritual of the four Masonic ceremonies is beyond the scope of this book. There are, however, a number of books available on the subject on the market: I have highlighted one or two in the Bibliography to enable interested readers to explore this particular aspect further. What is important to point out is that the ritual is learned, by heart, by all the officers of the lodge. Not unexpectedly, the Master has the largest part to learn. Each of the four Masonic

Above and opposite: **The layout of the Grand Temple is similar to all Lodge Rooms, save that it is 37m. long, 27m. wide and 62m. high and has a capacity in excess of 1,600.**

ceremonies lasts between twenty and forty minutes and even as short one-act plays they can be very demanding on the participants, most of whom will not have had any previous experience of acting or indeed learning lines. Whereas at one time it was expected that the Master carried out all of the work from the Chair, such are the pressure of modern life that these days it is not unusual for the Master's part to be shared with one or two willing Past Masters.

After the Meeting

Once the lodge has been closed, the members and guests retire to change out of their Masonic regalia and have a drink at the bar prior to the Festive Board. The arrangements for the Festive Board are fairly formal and there is usually some form of seating plan. Not unreasonably, the Festive Board is presided over by the Master under the ever-watchful eye of the Director of Ceremonies; though practice does vary and in London it tends to be the Immediate Past Master who coordinates matters at dinner. Even if there is no formal seating plan, the positions of the Master and the two Wardens are fixed. If all are seated at one table the Master will sit in the

centre with the Senior Warden at the right hand end and the Junior Warden at the left. If the tables are arranged as sprigs, then the Master will be in the centre of the top table with the Senior Warden on the end of the sprig on the far right and the Junior Warden on the end of the far left sprig.

The dinner may be punctuated with various wine-takings. The participants when announced by the Director of Ceremonies stand to acknowledge each other and drink a toast. For example, the Master may take wine with his Wardens and then with all of the Brethren present.

At the conclusion of dinner there will be a number of formal toasts that are usually concluded with Masonic Fire. The main toasts are those to the Queen, the Grand Master, the Provincial Grand Master and the Master of the Lodge. Other toasts may include those to the Grand Officers, Provincial Grand Officers, the Candidate and the Visitors.

Some of the toasts will receive either no formal response or perhaps a short response, others such as those to the Master or Visitors may result in a more lengthy reply. Regrettably not all Freemasons are natural after-dinner speakers and Freemasons, being usually good mannered, are too polite to advise them accordingly.

Masonic Fire is believed to have been copied from the practice followed at military dinners, and is said to replicate the firing of guns in salute. It derives from the time when Masonic lodges were held round a table in a tavern. After the toast had been given, the glass was drained of its contents and banged on the table, in appreciation of what had been heard and to show that the glass was empty and ready to be re-filled. In time, no doubt because of sustained breakages, special firing glasses began to be made – too small to drink out of but with a heavy bulbous bottom that meant that they could be safely banged on the table without fear of breaking – whilst the wine continued to be served in traditional drinking glasses. As not all lodges have firing glasses, the action and noise is simulated in most lodges by clapping the hands to a particular rhythm.

I for one have always found it amusing that some lodge Directors of Ceremonies become almost apoplectic in ensuring that waiting staff are removed from the dining room before the toasts are fired so they cannot hear what is going on; apparently completely oblivious to the fact that they can hear perfectly well from the other side of the door and probably know the method of firing better than those in the room, having heard it every night of the week.

How do I become a Freemason?

Some thirty years ago, for reasons that are still far from clear, the expectation was that a potential candidate was expected to make the first move and ask his prospective Proposer for more details and indicate that he was interested in joining. The general feeling was that it was not proper to proselytise or actively canvas for candidates. This often led to contradictory situations, whereby a candidate wanted to become a Freemason but thought it was inappropriate to ask his potential Proposer; and his potential Proposer thinking it was not appropriate to suggest to the candidate that he would make an excellent member.

One very useful method of testing the water was to invite likely members to the ubiquitous Ladies' Night. The Ladies' Night, which still prevails in many Masonic lodges, was an annual dinner-dance, at which the Master presided but it was his wife, or lady, who was the guest of honour. In many ways it was seen as a thank-you and recognition of the fact that the men could not carry out their Freemasonry without the support of their ladies. There is no doubting that in many instances it was the social highlight of the year and in some instances continues to be so, particularly outside London. In London the situation has materially altered – for no better reason than cost. A Ladies' Night in London is almost prohibitively expensive, not just with the high cost of dining, room hire and a live band; but also the drink-driving laws necessitate a taxi home or an hotel stay overnight. This is the main reason why a number of lodges started to have Ladies' Weekends, rather than Ladies' Nights, in places such as Bournemouth or Eastbourne and even further afield, as the overall cost was very similar and better value for money. Having said that, dinner-dances are very passé these days and not the type of social event that is likely to appeal to a younger generation. Nevertheless, Freemasons are by their very nature conservative and hence the Ladies' Night or Weekend is here to stay for some time yet.

The situation these days regarding potential members is very different and candidates are actively encouraged to approach prospective Proposers to indicate that they are interested in becoming members. A number of lodges have even set up websites with contact details for potential candidates, and adverts in local newspapers encouraging new recruits are not unusual. Lodges also hold 'open-days', where members of the local community are encouraged to attend together with their spouse or partner and where the basics of Freemasonry are explained together with the opportunity of seeing how a Lodge Room is laid out. Such occasions usually generate some candidates coming forward with a desire to find out more. Likewise Grand Lodge have launched a very successful University scheme, whereby a local lodge is linked with the university in the area – this has proved to be a good and reliable means of recruitment. Indeed the Grand Lodge website provides an excellent, readable introductory booklet for anybody who is thinking of becoming a Freemason – but then I would say that, wouldn't I?

All organisations are having difficulties in recruiting new members, especially those in the 25 to 45 age bracket and Freemasonry is no exception in that regard. However, numbers are not everything and care is still taken to ensure that individual candidates are suitable for Freemasonry and indeed that Freemasonry is suitable for the candidate himself. All candidates will be interviewed prior to their candidature being voted on by members of the lodge. It is important that candidates know as much as possible about Freemasonry and what is expected of them before being formally considered. The critical elements are a belief in a Supreme Being, being of good character, the support of one's wife or partner and the ability to be able to afford it in terms of finance and time.

One of the reasons why there is a paucity of candidates in the 25 to 45 age bracket is fairly simple and quite obvious. It is the time when the majority of young men, and indeed women, are thinking of getting married, starting a family and developing their careers. There is much merit in a Freemason joining in his early twenties and then putting Masonry on hold until such a time as his career and family are more settled before taking it up again. In this day and age there are not too many bosses or managers who would take kindly to someone wanting to leave work early to attend a Masonic meeting; nor would their wife or partner excuse supermarket duties or the taxi service for ballet classes or soccer training on a Saturday morning.

Being of good character is important in Freemasonry. There are not many membership organisations that are prepared to suspend or expel members for committing a criminal offence – and that includes the House of Lords! Whilst there are the usual safeguards and appeals procedures in place, it is true to say that any Freemason convicted of an offence that merits a custodial or community service sentence will be expelled from the Craft; and similarly it would be a bar to becoming a member. Disciplinary matters are dealt with on a Provincial basis and there is some variation when it comes to dealing with purely Masonic offences, but a Provincial Grand Master does have the power to suspend a member for committing a lesser criminal offence such as drink-driving and regrettably some members have found themselves suspended from their lodge for a period of twelve months whilst serving a similar length of suspension from driving.

As a lodge is to all intents and purposes a club, if you are interesting in joining you will need to have a Proposer and Seconder. There are, as has already been indicated, a number of ways that this might be achieved. If you know someone who is a Freemason, you now know that you can approach him directly to find out more at first hand. Most Freemasons will be able to fill in any details lacking in this book. He should be able to tell you which lodges may best suit you. Some lodges are known as 'closed' lodges where membership is restricted. For example a 'School Lodge' may only accept members who are former pupils or present and past members of staff. If you are not eligible to join his particular Lodge, he is more than likely able to recommend one that will and put you in touch with the Secretary or other senior member to take matters forward. The Internet has already been alluded to and is a veritable mine of information for anybody wishing to find out about Freemasonry for whatever reason.

How much does it cost to be a Freemason?

There are several elements that make up the total cost of being a Freemason. The lodge will charge a one-off Joining or Initiation fee – anything from £50 to £500; which, like the annual subscription, will contain elements that need to paid to both the Provincial Grand Lodge and to Grand Lodge. Every Freemason is automatically a member of the Freemasons' Grand Charity; and his annual subscription – in the order of £110 to £150 per year – includes a compulsory element, currently £17.00, that goes to the Charity. On top of the annual subscription is the cost of dining. This is dependent on the number of times a lodge meets during the course of a year and the venue where the members choose to dine. Most lodges meet four or five times a year but some do meet ten or eleven times a year. Dining may cost as little as £15 (excluding wine) to in excess of £75 in central London. There is the cost of regalia, that changes with the status of the Freemason as he progresses through the ranks. At the time of writing, the basic Master Mason's apron will cost £40; a Master's collar and apron £70; Provincial Grand Officer's collar and apron £120; whilst that of a Grand Officer will cost something over £400. Variable costs include such things as visiting and charity. A Mason can invite a fellow Mason from another lodge to attend a meeting and to stay for dinner afterwards. In fact inter-visiting plays a great part in Freemasonry. The visits are usually reciprocated and a number of Masons enjoy their Freemasonry so much that they will always invite one or more guests to their own lodge on a regular basis. In some Provinces it is traditional that the Master of a Lodge, during his year in office, visits all the other lodges in the Province. A heavy duty in terms of cost, time and body weight, given the number of Masonic meals that are likely to be consumed! There is usually a charity collection at the conclusion of every Masonic meeting. This can take place in the Lodge Room or afterwards at the Festive Board. The amount donated is a matter entirely at the discretion of the individual, but is unlikely to be less than £1.00 or more than £20.00. Lodges have woken up to the tax situation in recent years and more often than not the donation is placed in an envelope on the front of which the necessary tax declaration can be signed, thereby enabling the lodge to claim a further amount for the benefit of charity from Her Majesty's Revenue and Customs. It is also quite likely that some form of raffle might be held at the Festive Board to raise funds for charity; that is in addition to, rather than instead of, the Charity collection. Such is human nature that the raffle more often than not raises more than the charity collection.

There are five main Masonic Charities: the four Craft Charities – The Grand Charity, The Royal Masonic Benevolent Institution (RMBI), The Royal Masonic Trust for Girls and Boys (RMTGB) and the Masonic Samaritan Fund (MSF); and in addition one of the other Orders of Freemasonry – the Mark – has its own charity known as the Mark Benevolent Fund, which celebrates its centenary in 2018. The charities derive no income from outside funding, such as the National Lottery. The sums raised are therefore almost entirely from the pockets of members. Every Province can expect to host a Festival for one of the five Charities every eleven years. The sums raised are not inconsiderable and the expectation is that every member will contribute something in the order of £500 over the five-year period that the Province will be raising funds.

Being a Freemason is not at the cheapest end of the scale of leisure activities but nor is it by any means the most expensive. The one thing that does differentiate it from other social activities is the level of commitment that is necessary to make it worthwhile and meaningful.

How do Freemasons get the best jobs?

We now get to the nub of why you may have bought this book. What pecuniary advantages are there to be gained as a Freemason? Well, sorry to disappoint you. Having read through the book thus far, you should be beginning to realise that there are *no* pecuniary advantages to be gained by becoming a Freemason. To get the best jobs you do not have to be a Freemason.

In fact in some areas of local government it is a positive disadvantage. It is only comparatively recently that two judgements in the European Court of Human Rights, brought on behalf of Italian Freemasons, found that it was discriminatory to be asked to declare membership of a non-secret society. As a consequence, action taken by Grand Lodge has resulted in a number of organisations having to delete from their application forms phrases such as: 'Are you a member of any Secret Societies such as the Freemasons?' In 2009, it was decided that members of the Judiciary would no longer have to declare their Masonic membership after Grand Lodge indicated it may seek judicial review of the policy. People and organizations that are antagonistic towards Freemasonry consistently fail to differentiate between secrecy on the one hand and privacy on the other. There is still discrimination against Freemasons in the field of employment. So the advice to anyone considering becoming a Freemason in order to find a better job is short and succinct – don't!

Wild accusations and allegations can, and often are, made on a variety of fronts regarding Freemasons and the pernicious nature of Freemasonry. These allegations, which continue to appear from time to time, are always entirely anecdotal. No concrete evidence that could be tested in a court of law or through independent scrutiny, and which substantiates any such accusations, has ever been forthcoming. If any reader has contrary information I would be delighted to hear from them.

In so far as the job question is concerned it is worth looking at some of the logistics behind the assertion and to ask oneself How? and Why? In the public sector most if not all jobs are advertised in the public domain with a very detailed job and person specification. The selection process is normally carried out by some form of panel, and it would not be unusual if that panel contained at least one woman. So the first question is, how can a candidate influence the appointment process on the basis that he is a Freemason?

Well, I suppose he could put Freemasonry on his application form as one of his hobbies or interests. I have no doubt that might raise one or two interesting talking points if he got to the interview stage. He could pepper his application form with snippets lifted from the ritual, which might be picked up by another Freemason – it would certainly make the application form extraordinary reading.

A ludicrous and impossible scenario would be for the candidate to try to obtain the names of those on the panel, to see if any of them were Freemasons. The names of lodge members are often found on the back of the summons and agenda for every meeting of a lodge, which is sent to every member some two weeks prior to a meeting. I suppose, in theory, he could obtain one of these by writing to all the Lodge Secretaries in the area, asking for copies of their respective summonses or alternatively he could write to the Provincial Secretary for the copies – though in neither case would such information be sent to a total stranger. An alternative strategy would be to contact the Provincial Secretary to ask for a copy of the Provincial Year Book. That publication will normally contain the names of the Provincial Grand Officers; the problem here is that the person concerned may not have yet been through the Chair and hence not be a Provincial Officer. The same problem would arise if he bought a copy of the Grand Lodge Year Book that contains the names of all the Grand Officers.

There is of course another major flaw in this nonsensical scenario – the panel member could live in one Province and belong to a lodge in a neighbouring Province – I am not sure how one begins to get round that issue. What I have described is patently a complete nonsense but something that the detractors of Freemasonry, who are great believers in conspiracy theories, seem to relish.

It reinforces my belief that if one phones the local golf club and asks for the contact details of an individual member, you would be given short shrift on the grounds of privacy. Yet if the same question is asked of a lodge or Provincial Secretary and a similar answer is given, then information has been denied on the grounds of secrecy!

All of this does not address the other point of Why? Why should a member of an appointments panel give favourable consideration to a candidate who also happens to be a Freemason? What advantage is to be gained by doing so? If appointed, he has still to deliver the goods and if he fails to do so, then not unreasonably questions would be asked.

The same applies to the private sector. It is rare in a company of any size for appointments to be made by any one individual. The same hypothesis applies as to what may be gained by favouring a particular candidate for no other reason that he is a Freemason.

What *can* be said about Freemasonry is that it is probably one of the earliest forms of 'networking'. On that basis it may well be, and particularly in a smaller town, that members in the same profession or area of employment know each other. Useful if you need a plumber or electrician, not so useful if the man concerned does not do a good job or overcharges you. The same principle applies if a sole-trader employs a fellow Freemason on the same basis; difficult to deal with, if it does not work out. Needless to say all that has been said in respect of networking applies equally well to membership of other organisations such as Rotary, a golf club, Knights of Columba and others.

Having said that, I have to admit that there *are* ways that Freemasonry will improve your employment prospects and thus help get you the best job by developing your 'interchangeable management skills'. As a Freemason you will have the opportunity to improve your memory, hone your inter-personal skills, speak in public, practice social skills, learn about wine and food, be of service to others, dress properly and understand the importance of making and fulfilling a commitment.

How do Freemasons always get their Planning Permissions through?

The short answer is – in exactly the same way as any other member of the public. The scenario detailed above regarding applying for jobs within the public sector applies equally well to Planning Permission. In theory, one would need to 'nobble' either the appropriate Planning Officer(s) or member(s) of the Planning Committee. In summary, not all Planning Officers are men – let alone Freemasons – and the same applies to the members of the Planning Committee. I have to confess, other than the ridiculous scenario I painted above, I would not know where to start. In the final analysis it should be pointed out that any attempt to use Freemasonry for such a purpose would amount to a criminal offence for both parties; the result being not only some form of custodial sentence but also expulsion from Freemasonry.

How do Freemasons avoid getting caught by the Police?

I am afraid the same applies – they don't. It is difficult to imagine any circumstances where Freemasonry could be used to prevent due process taking place. The fact of the matter is that within a structured organisation such as the police, everybody has a superior officer to which they are accountable. There is always some form of audit trail. Even if a police officer wished to let a fellow Freemason off some alleged crime, the paperwork involved would be such as to make it almost impossible. Once again, the consequences for both parties if caught far outweigh any advantage likely to be gained.

How do Freemasons manage to get off in Court?

I am sure you have got the drift by now. In March 1997, the House of Commons Home Affairs Committee reported on the results of an investigation into Freemasonry in the Police and the Judiciary. Certain members of the Committee appeared to be convinced that Freemasons are members of some form of sinister secret society who unjustly exert unfair influence in promoting and defending other Freemasons. They seemed to believe that Freemasons are engaged in a conspiracy to hide wrongdoing by other Freemasons; apparently abetted by Judges, who exonerate criminals, whom they recognise as fellow Freemasons from secret signs made from the dock. A non sequitur, given that Freemasons should (in theory) never appear in court, since some members of the Committee appeared equally convinced that policemen who are Freemasons fail to take appropriate action against other Freemasons who have committed crimes.

The Committee took evidence from a wide range of people, including the Lord Chancellor, the Magistrates Association, the Association of Chief Police Officers, the Judiciary, the Bar Council, the Crown Prosecution Service and a number of individuals.

The long and short of it is that none of the organizations detailed above offered any evidence that Freemasonry caused any problems, exercised any undue influence or had any record of such issues arising.

Notwithstanding the lack of evidence, the Committee agreed the following: 'We recommend that police officers, magistrates, judges and crown prosecutors should be required to register membership of any secret society and that the record should be publicly available.'

One satisfying fact, on my part, is that even given the openly anti-Masonic stance of Chris Mullin, the Chairman, he and his Committee were not able to find any conclusive evidence of the adverse influence of Freemasonry in the Police and the Judiciary.

There followed in 1999 a second report by another Home Affairs Committee, this time on Freemasonry in Public Life. The findings of that Committee, which started where the previous Committee had left off, included the following:

> *We repeat the point made in the previous Report: there is a great deal of unjustified paranoia about Freemasonry, but Freemasons, with their obsessive secrecy, are partly to blame for this.*
>
> *We are also aware that there is a widespread belief that improper Masonic influence does play a part in public life. Most of these allegations are impossible to prove. Where they can be carefully examined, they usually prove unfounded. It is clear, however, from some of the examples cited in this Report, and the previous Report, that there are cases where allegations of improper Masonic influence may well be justified.*

If it is *that* clear that there are cases '…where allegations of improper Masonic influence may well be justified' – all I will say is, why was the opportunity not taken to investigate them?

What is clear is that the various allegations made against Freemasons and the 'pernicious' influence of Freemasonry appear to be based on warped perception and not fact.

For those who have already made their minds up about the so-called evils of Freemasonry, nothing in the preceding section will make one iota of difference to them. To those with an open mind, perhaps they have been given food for thought. For any Freemasons reading this book – whilst they may not need any convincing, at least they now have a little more information on the subject.

Who are these Freemasons and why join if there is no pecuniary advantage?

Freemasons in England are, by and large, white, middle-aged and middle class men. The average age of a Freemason is a little over sixty. Although predominantly white, there are considerable numbers of Freemasons from different ethnic backgrounds, both at home and abroad, who are members of the Craft. Grand Lodge does not keep statistics relating to the ethnic origin of members, any more than it does relating to those of religion. The term middle class is not meant in any pejorative sense and indeed it could be argued that the term is now outdated. Whilst the occupation or profession of candidates is noted on the application form for membership, I have not carried out any detailed analysis or classification and hence only offer a personal impression. The composition of a lodge varies widely and there is no such thing as a typical lodge. The whole ethic in relation to Freemasonry, ethnicity, religion and occupation is best summed up in Rudyard Kipling's poem about his Mother Lodge. The lodge into which a Freemason is initiated is known as his Mother Lodge, even though he may well become a Joining Member of other lodges in the future.

The reasons why men choose to become Freemasons are various, many and to a large extent unquantifiable. Whilst great emphasis is placed on recruitment of new Freemasons, retention of existing members is just as important. Freemasonry is not for everybody. My advice has always been – if you are interested, join. It is the only way that you will really find out what it is all about. By the same token, having joined, if you do not like it – leave. It is not insignificant that some twenty per cent of new members leave within five years of joining; those that stay usually remain members for a considerable number of years. The reasons for leaving are not easy to determine. Lodges do try to carry out 'exit surveys' but as often as not, the real reason is not always clear. Rest assured that those who do leave are not pursued, their names do not go onto some international blacklist, nor are they dealt with in the same way as William Morgan is alleged to have been dealt with!

Meeting on the Level

I like to think that men become Masons for good and honourable reasons. The two incidents that sum up for me what Freemasonry is or should be about are those relating to a story about Theodore Roosevelt, the 26th President of the United States of America and his gardener, W.M. James Duthie; and the episode involving Generals Hancock and Armistead, who fought on opposing sides at the Battle of Gettysburg during the American Civil War.

President Theodore Roosevelt is one of fourteen Presidents of the USA to have been a Freemason. He was initiated in January 1901 into a Lodge in Oyster Bay, New York. At a White House lunch, the question of Masonry came up and it transpired that every man present was a Mason. The President remarked that one of the aspects of Freemasonry that appealed to him was the fact that it brought men together from very different stations of life. 'Do you know,' said the President, 'that the Master of my Lodge is just a working man, a gardener for one of my neighbours in Oyster Bay; but when I visit Matinecock Lodge he is my boss, and I must stand up when he orders me, and sit down when he tells me, and not speak unless he allows me.' W. M. James Duthie was the gardener referred to by the President, a Scot who was Master of Matinecock Lodge for three years during President Roosevelt's first administration in 1902 to 1904. He was the Senior Warden of the Lodge when Roosevelt was raised. The conversation was witnessed by the Revd Alexander G. Russell, Pastor of the Presbyterian Church at Oyster Bay, who was present at the lunch and published the story in a memoire dated 1919.

Having been a Freemason for over thirty years, one of the aspects that appeals to me is the opportunity to mix and socialise with a very eclectic group of men from very diverse backgrounds. In Masonic jargon 'one meets on the level' whilst in the lodge, but social order is restored again once the meeting has ended.

The second incident is commemorated by a monument on the battlefield at Gettysburg, presented by the Grand Lodge of Pennsylvania in 1993 and dedicated as a memorial to the Freemasons of the Confederacy. As the inscriptions on either side of the monument state:

Their unique bonds of friendship enabled them to remain, a brotherhood undivided, even as they fought as a divided nation, faithfully supporting the respective governments under which they lived.

and

Union General Winfield Scott Hancock and Confederate General Lewis Addison Armistead were personal friends and members of the Masonic Fraternity.

Although they had served and fought side by side in the United States Army prior to the Civil war, Armistead refused to raise his sword against his fellow Southerners and joined the Confederate Army in 1861.

Both Hancock and Armistead fought heroically in the previous twenty-seven months of the war. They were destined to meet at Gettysburg.

During Pickett's Charge, Armistead led his men gallantly, penetrating Hancock's line. Ironically, when Armistead was mortally wounded, Hancock was also wounded.

Depicted in the sculpture is Union Captain Henry Bingham, a Mason and staff assistant to General Hancock, himself wounded rendering aid to the fallen Confederate General. Armistead is shown handing his watch and personal effects to be taken to his friend, Union General Hancock.

Hancock survived the war and died in 1886. Armistead died at Gettysburg, July 5, 1863. Captain Bingham attained the rank of general and later served 32 years in the United States House of Representatives. He was known as the 'Father of the House'.

The values of Masonry include honesty, integrity and commitment. The incident described above shows that even at times of considerable strife, such as war, it is still possible to act honourably and with a considerable degree of humanity.

Freemasonry strives to make good men better.

The 'Friend to Friend Masonic Memorial' on the battlefield at Gettysburg, presented by the Grand Lodge of Pennsylvania in 1993 and dedicated to the Freemasons of the Union and the Confederacy. The inscription states:

'Their unique bonds of friendship enabled them to remain, a brotherhood undivided, even as they fought as a divided nation, faithfully supporting the respective governments under which they lived.'

PART II

....

An A to Z of Freemasonry

*S*ome topics concerning Freemasonry deserve to be covered in more *depth. The format adopted in Part II is encyclopaedic and laid out in alphabetical order. Having been a Freemason for many years it is difficult to decide what is likely to appeal to non-Masons wanting to find out more about the subject. Adopting this format enables readers to dip in and out on an eclectic basis, having decided for themselves what is of most interest to them.*

Advertising Membership

Having taken his Third Degree, every Mason receives a Certificate from Grand Lodge. It comes folded and is presented during a lodge meeting. The new Mason is informed during the presentation that it constitutes a Masonic Passport and should be taken with him when he visits another lodge to prove his membership. He is also advised that the reason the Certificate comes folded is that it should not be displayed so as to advertise his Masonic membership. This sets the tone in so far as advertising one's membership is concerned. Having said that, many Masons in this country wear discreet Masonic jewellery such as cufflinks, tiepin or ring – usually bearing an image of the square and compasses. Lapel pins

Fred has gone over the top again I see – **even the iconic emblem of Freemasonry is capable of generating a smile.**

have become increasingly common – a favourite being a 'forget-me-knot', that was originally worn by German Masons as a sign of recognition when Freemasonry was proscribed in that country. Other examples of Masonic jewellery can be found through the Internet. However, the obvious still needs to be pointed out – that just because someone is wearing Masonic jewellery it does not make him a Mason.

The low-key advertising in this country is in stark contrast with the situation in the United States, where baseball caps, tee shirts, jackets and the like (including car number plates) can be found proudly bearing the square and compasses.

Affinity Lodges or Interest Lodges

Lodges are set up or 'founded' for a variety of reasons. A large number of lodges are established because the Founders share an interest outside Masonry – such as Scouting, Round Table or Rotary – and because they enjoy their Masonry so much they wish to bring the two aspects closer together.

Although they exist in all parts of the country, the majority of these lodges are in London, where of some 1,400 lodges getting on for 500 can be described as interest or affinity lodges, which cater for the many interest groups. These can be categorised as follows:

Building	Architects, Surveyors.
Education	Universities, Public School Lodges Council, other Headmasters' Conference Schools, other Schools and Colleges, Schoolmasters, Training Colleges.
Engineering	Civil, Electrical, Gas, Mechanical, Sanitary.
Finance	Accountancy, Banking, Insurance, Stockbroking.
Food and Drink	Bakers and Confectioners, Butchers, Fishmongers, Licensed Victuallers, Teetotallers.
Geographical	Commonwealth Lodges Association, Overseas, UK Counties and Regions, London – City, London – Wards.
Law	Barristers, Solicitors.
Livery Companies	
Medical	Association of Medical, University and Legal Lodges.
Military	Circuit of Service Lodges.
Paper, Printing & Publishing	
Public Sector	Civil Service, Local Government, Fire Brigade, Police, Post Office, Water Board.
Sport and Recreation	Sports, Recreations, Youth Movements.
The Arts	Literary, Musical, Theatrical.
Transport	Aviation, Railways, Shipping.
Miscellaneous	Clubs and Societies, Ecclesiastical, Funereal, Iron and Steel, Sales Managers, Secretarial, Telegraph and Cables.

To give some flavour of the range of actual lodges and interests, the list below is taken from the Miscellaneous category:

Burgoyne No. 902 (Connaught Club – under 35s), Lombardian No. 2348 (Pawnbrokers), Sir Walter Raleigh No. 2432 (Tobacco), Hortus No. 2469 (Florists), Alfred Newton No. 2686 (Harrods), Commercial Travellers No. 2795, Carbon No. 2910 (Coal Merchants), Rostrum No. 3037 (Auctioneers), Arts & Crafts No. 3387 (Designers), Renaissance No. 3408 (Decorators), Inventions No. 3776 (Patent Agents), Armament No. 3898 (Munitions), St Vedast No. 4033 (Soft Goods), Mercurius No. 4262 (Drapers), Lodge of Good Companions No. 6091 (Plastics), Savoy No. 8356 (Hotel staff), Prior Walter No. 8687 (Order of St John of Jerusalem).

It should also be borne in mind that many of the lodges detailed (as their Lodge Number indicates) were founded some years ago and originally would have been known as 'closed' lodges where membership is restricted to a particular category of member. For example, a 'School Lodge' may only accept members who are former pupils or present and past members of staff. However, in recent years many lodges have decided to 'open' membership beyond the original objectives of the Founders. For instance, Maguncor Lodge No. 3806 was formed in 1917 and all the original members and Founders were officers in the Machine Gun Corps. I am sure it will be appreciated that there are not too many potential members around today who would satisfy the initial criterion, so the Lodge decided to 'open up' its membership some time ago but is pleased and proud to be able to retain its original links and traditions.

American Freemasonry

Freemasonry spread overseas very quickly after it was formalised in England in 1717. It is claimed that a lodge met in King's Chapel, Boston as early as the 1720s. Benjamin Franklin in his *Pennsylvania Gazette* of 1730 notes that lately several Masonic lodges have been erected within the Province. In 1733 Henry Price, who emigrated to Boston in 1723, was appointed 'Provincial Grand Master of New England and Dominions and Territories thereunto belonging'. On 30 July 1733, at a meeting held at The Bunch of Grapes Tavern in Boston, St John's Lodge was formed, making it the oldest formally constituted Lodge in the Americas.

Benjamin Franklin, who initially wrote some less than flattering pieces about Masonry, saw the error of his ways: he was initiated in 1731 and in 1734, whilst he was Master of his Lodge, published in Philadelphia the first Masonic book in America – an American version of Anderson's *Constitutions*.

Freemasons played a significant part in the early years of the United States. Of the fifty-six signatories of the Declaration of Independence, nine were Freemasons and of the thirty-nine who signed the US Constitution, thirteen were Freemasons.

Prominent revolutionaries who were also Freemasons include George Washington, John Hancock, Paul Revere and the Marquis de Lafayette.

One aspect of American Freemasonry which makes it different from English Freemasonry is its extension to the rest of the family. DeMolay International is an organisation for boys aged 12 to 21;

Benjamin Franklin, responsible for the publication of the first Masonic book in America and Grand Master of Pennsylvania.

modelled on Masonic lines, it is sponsored by a Masonic body and often meets in a Masonic Lodge Room. Job's Daughters and the International Order of the Rainbow for Girls are Masonic-sponsored youth organisations for girls and young women aged 10 to 20 who are related to a Mason. They stress the importance of helping others through charity and service projects.

Aprons

Stonemasons traditionally wear long, leather aprons that are tied with a loop at the front with the ends hanging loose. This is replicated in Freemasonry, albeit with a smaller apron, traditionally made of white lambskin with a triangular flap. The type of apron worn designates the rank of the wearer.

On being initiated, an Entered Apprentice wears a plain white, lambskin apron – the badge of innocence; on being passed to the Second Degree he wears a white lambskin apron adorned with two blue rosettes, and on being raised to the Third Degree, three blue rosettes with the apron edged in light blue, moiré silk. On being installed as the Master of a Lodge the rosettes are replaced with silver levels.

The apron changes once Provincial rank is achieved, with levels in gold, the apron edged in dark blue, moiré silk and the rank of the holder depicted in an embroidered roundel in the centre of the apron.

Appointment to Grand Rank results in the apron becoming more elaborate, with the rank of the holder embroidered into the centre of the lambskin and considerable amounts of gold braid embroidery.

Once a Mason has been installed as a Worshipful Master he is also entitled to wear a Past Master's Collar of light blue, moiré silk appended with a jewel depicting his rank – a square and compasses. A Provincial or Grand Officer will wear a collar of dark blue, moiré silk with a jewel appended to it denoting his rank.

Church

The relationship between Freemasonry and the established Churches has never been an easy one. The antipathy of the Roman Catholic Church towards Freemasonry is long-standing and goes back almost as far as Freemasonry itself. As early as 1738 Pope Clement XII issued a Papal Bull *In Eminenti Apostolatus Specula* banning Catholics from becoming Freemasons.

> *...Now it has come to Our ears, and common gossip has made clear, that certain Societies, Companies, Assemblies, Meetings, Congregations or Conventicles called in the popular tongue Liberi Muratori or Francs Massons or by other names according to the various languages, are*

spreading far and wide and daily growing in strength; and men of any Religion or sect, satisfied with the appearance of natural probity, are joined together, according to their laws and the statutes laid down for them, by a strict and unbreakable bond which obliges them, both by an oath upon the Holy Bible and by a host of grievous punishment, to an inviolable silence about all that they do in secret together…

A number of Popes have pursued the same argument, some more vehemently than others, but perhaps most notably Pope Leo XIII in his Encyclical of 1884.

Whilst this is not the time or place for a discourse on the reasons for 250 years of antipathy on the part of the Roman Catholic Church, I will quote from parts of that Encyclical which summarise the various issues that appear to affect the Church as far as Freemasonry is concerned:

…At this period, however, the partisans of evil seems to be combining together, and to be struggling with united vehemence, led on or assisted by that strongly organized and widespread association called the Freemasons. No longer making any secret of their purposes, they are now boldly rising up against God Himself. They are planning the destruction of holy Church publicly and openly, and this with the set purpose of utterly despoiling the nations of Christendom…

…this apostolic see denounced the sect of the Freemasons, and publicly declared its constitution, as contrary to law and right, to be pernicious no less to Christendom than to the State; and it forbade any one to enter the society, under the penalties which the Church is wont to inflict upon exceptionally guilty persons…

…they easily deceive the simple-minded and the heedless, and can induce a far greater number to become members. Again, as all who offer themselves are received whatever may be their form of religion, they thereby teach the great error of this age – that a regard for religion should be held as an indifferent matter, and that all religions are alike. This manner of reasoning is calculated to bring about the ruin of all forms of religion, and especially of the Catholic religion, which, as it is the only one that is true…

…With the greatest unanimity the sect of the Freemasons also endeavours to take to itself the education of youth. They think that they can easily mould to their opinions that soft and pliant age, and bend it whither they will; and that nothing can be more fitted than this to enable them to bring up the youth of the State after their own plan…

> *…Their chief dogmas are so greatly and manifestly at variance with reason that nothing can be more perverse. To wish to destroy the religion and the Church which God Himself has established, and whose perpetuity He insures by His protection, and to bring back after a lapse of eighteen centuries the manners and customs of the pagans, is signal folly and audacious impiety…*

I have to confess that until I started to research this part of the book I had no idea of what lay behind the vehemence of the Roman Catholic Church's opposition to Freemasonry. There is a catalogue of similar denunciations by a number of Popes from 1738 up to the present day, including Benedict XIV (1751); Pius VII (1821); Leo XII (1825); Pius VIII (1829); Gregory XVI (1832); and Pius IX (1846 and 1869).

The ban on Freemasonry was formalized when it was enshrined in the Code of Canon Law of 1917. The two relevant Laws are:

> *Canon 2335: Affiliation With Masonic or Similar Societies. Those who join a Masonic sect or other societies of the same sort, which plot against the Church or against legitimate civil authority, incur ipso facto an excommunication simply reserved to the Holy See.*
>
> *Canon 1399: Books which hold duelling, suicide or divorce licit, or which, treating of Masonic sects and other such societies, contend that they are useful and not harmful to the Church and civil society are forbidden…*

The Code of Canon Law was revised and updated in 1983 and the relevant new Law did not specifically mention Freemasonry:

> *Canon 1374: A person who joins an association which plots against the Church is to be punished with a just penalty; one who promotes or takes office in such an association is to be punished…*

This led many Freemasons to believe that the ban had been lifted. However, to avoid any doubt, a statement was issued by the then Cardinal Joseph Ratzinger, before he became Pope Benedict XVI (now Pope Emeritus), which confirmed that:

> *…the Church's negative judgment in regard to Masonic association[s] remains unchanged since their principles have always been considered irreconcilable with the doctrine of the Church and therefore membership in them remains forbidden. The faithful who enrol in Masonic associations are in a state of grave sin and may not receive Holy Communion.*

My difficulty with the stance of the Roman Catholic Church in respect to Freemasonry is that I believe that the opposition and hostility stems from a fundamental misunderstanding of what Freemasonry is all about, particularly in this country where discussion of religion and politics in lodge is prohibited. There is little that I can add, other than to say that going right back to 1776 when Lord Robert Petre was elected Grand Master, Roman Catholics have continued to join the Craft in defiance of their Church's ruling.

In so far as other Christian denominations are concerned, the issue of Freemasonry and its compatibility with Christian teaching is a subject that surfaces now and again.

The Church of England last debated the issue back in 1987 when the General Synod considered a report *Freemasonry and Christianity: Are they compatible?* The final paragraph read:

> *This Report has identified a number of important issues on which, in the view of the Working Group, the General Synod will have to reflect as it considers 'the compatibility or otherwise of Freemasonry with Christianity'. The reflections of the Working Group itself reveal understandable differences of opinion between those who are Freemasons and those who are not. Whilst the former fully agree that the Report shows that there are clear difficulties to be faced by Christians who are Freemasons, the latter are of the mind that the Report points to a number of very fundamental reasons to question the compatibility of Freemasonry and Christianity.*

The issue has not been formally discussed since then and circumstances and attitudes have changed since that time. The Most Revd Geoffrey Fisher, who retired in 1961, was both Archbishop of Canterbury and an active and prominent Mason. Freemasons in this country continue to give active support to the Church of England, not only in terms of their attendance in the congregation but also in the level of financial assistance donated towards the maintenance of the fabric of churches and cathedrals and the support of such initiatives as choral scholarships.

The Methodist Church debated the issue in 1985, when Methodist Freemasons were asked to reconsider their membership on the grounds that Freemasonry competed with Christian beliefs; but they did not go as far as placing a ban on membership.

A similar situation arose when in 1989 the general Assembly of the Church of Scotland decided that there were 'very real theological difficulties' in their members being Freemasons but again stopped short of a ban.

I do not know why there was a hiatus in the discussion and debate about Freemasonry and membership of the various Churches during the period 1985-

1989, but nothing of that intensity has taken place since and Freemasons appear to continue to practice their faith in Church and be active Freemasons without any obvious conflict of interest

Co-Freemasonry

Co-Masonry, or Mixed Masonry, is worked in lodges composed of both men and women. By the end of the nineteenth century, the Masonic scene in France was very complicated, with a proliferation of Grand Lodges and groups continually breaking away to become independent. One such lodge, *Les Libres Penseurs* (the Free Thinkers), – originally descended from the *Grande Loge de France* – when they failed to get permission from their governing body, decided to go it alone and initiate women.

Maria Desraimes, an atheist and well-known feminist, was initiated into this Lodge in 1882. It was not until 1893 that she and others formed yet another Grand Lodge, but one which admitted women. This later became *La Grande Loge Symbolique Mixte Le Droit Humain. Le Droit Humain* in France did not use the Volume of the Sacred Law or make any reference to the Great Architect of the Universe in their rituals.

The Order was brought to England by the feminist and free-thinker Annie Besant, who had been initiated into it in Paris. She organised the formation in London of the Lodge of Human Duty No. 6 on 26 September 1902. The President of the Theosophical Society, she saw Freemasonry as a means to further the cause of universal brotherhood and Co-Masons, as they were called, were closely involved with the work of the this Society.

In contrast to the situation in France, Annie Besant negotiated with the governing body there for permission to use in England the Volume of the Sacred Law and for the recognition of the Great Architect of the Universe in the ritual.

In this country, the Order, formally known as The International Order of Co-Freemasonry, *Le Droit Human,* is now called The International Order of Freemasonry for Women and Men, *Le Droit Humain.*

The Order, which members of the United Grand Lodge of England are banned from joining or visiting, has continued to expand. Various groups have broken away over the years to form their own Orders. In 2001, following disagreements within the British Federation of *Le Droit Humain*, some members left to establish in this country The Grand Lodge of Freemasonry for Men and Women.

Colonial Freemasonry

After the first Grand Lodge was formalised in England in 1717 Freemasonry quickly spread to the other parts of the British Empire. This was partly through Travelling Warrants (the authority to start a lodge) granted to regiments of the British army, but also to Warrants granted locally to civil servants and civilians stationed in the various outposts of the Empire.

The first Provincial Grand Master for India was appointed as early as 1728 and the first lodges overseas include a lodge at Fort William, Calcutta, India – 1730; Lodge of the East, Calcutta, India – 1740; St John's Lodge, Boson, USA – 1733 and Solomon Lodge No. 1, Savannah, USA – 1734.

Freemasonry formed an important part of the social structure for those serving overseas. By way of example, in Singapore the first English lodge was formed in 1845. The Singapore Cricket Club was set up shortly afterwards in 1852 and initially used to store its equipment on the Lodge premises – no doubt because of common membership between the two bodies.

Cost of Freemasonry

The costs of Freemasonry may be broken down into a number of categories: Initiation/Joining fee, annual subscriptions, dining, regalia and charity. The Initiation/Joining fees are each determined by individual lodges, as is the annual subscription. The latter is dependent on a number of factors, not least the cost of the meeting place. The annual subscription also contains elements for general administration and payment of annual dues to both the Province and Grand Lodge, together with a compulsory element (currently £17 p.a.) to be paid to the Grand Charity of which every Freemason is a member. Dining costs are, if you pardon the pun, a moveable feast. The cost varies considerably up and down the country and according to the venue at which the lodge chooses to dine.

Regalia gets more complicated, and hence more expensive, the higher one progresses up the Masonic ladder. Charity, which is a central tenet of Freemasonry, is entirely a matter for the individual Mason and the amount donated should not be to the detriment to himself or his family. As already stated, £17 to the Grand Charity is included in the annual subscription; in addition a collection is taken during every lodge meeting, though sometimes this is deferred to the dinner afterwards. The amount donated on each occasion is a matter for the individual concerned but is unlikely to be less than £1. On an annual basis, it is likely that a Mason may be asked to contribute to the Master's List which enables each year's Worshipful Master to suggest a particular charity to which all the monies collected during his year in office are donated.

The five main Masonic Charities each have an Annual Festival, hosted by one of the forty-four out of the forty-seven different Masonic Provinces (Guernsey & Alderney, Jersey and London are not included). It means that each Masonic Province can expect to host a Charity Festival every eleven years. Most Provinces limit the money-raising activities to a five year period and the normal expectation is that a member should try to achieve the minimum status of what is known as a 'Steward'

– by donating a sum of £500 during the five year period. Other levels such as Vice-Patron, Patron and Grand Patron can be achieved by donating larger amounts.

The various costs at the time of writing are summarised below but, bearing in mind the possible variations, they should only be taken as an indication of the order of cost. However, it is very unlikely that the annual cost of being a Craft Mason comes anywhere near that of an annual subscription to even the most modest of golf clubs.

Initiation/Joining Fee	£50 to £500	
Annual Subscriptions	£110 to £150	
Dining	£15 to £75 in central London	
Regalia	Mason's apron	£40
	Master's collar and apron	£70
	Provincial Grand Officer's collar and apron	£120
	Grand Officer	£400
Charity	£17.00 included in Annual Subscription	
	*£1.00+ per meeting	
	*£1.00+ per annum towards the **Master's List	
	*£500+: suggested amount to be donated usually over a five year period towards a Province's contribution to one of the five major Masonic Charity Festivals	

*   *The amount donated by an individual Mason is at his discretion and entirely voluntary and should take account of his personal circumstances*

** *Many Lodges have a system whereby donations are made during his year towards the 'Master's List' and at the end of the year the Master suggests which charities, whether Masonic or non-Masonic, should benefit.*

Craft Freemasonry
Craft Freemasonry consists of Three Degrees. A new member is initiated into the First Degree (an Entered Apprentice); passed to the Second Degree (a Fellowcraft) and raised to the Third Degree (a Master Mason). The word Craft is the generic term used for mainstream Freemasonry in this country. In the United States and in other parts of the world it is often refereed to as 'Blue' Masonry – in reference to the predominantly blue aprons worn by Freemasons during lodge meetings.

Dictators and Freemasonry
It is true to say that dictators have never really come to terms with Freemasonry, which they are convinced is part of some form of international conspiracy, closely allied

the Grand Procession of the Scald Miserable Masons Designed as they were Drawn up over against Somerset House, in the Strand, on the twenty Seventh of April An. 74

Above: **A procession of 'Scald Miserable Masons' in 1742 – an early attempt to ridicule and mock the public processions of Freemasons, an engraving by Antoine Benoist, printed in 1771.**

Left: **One of the earliest examples of public antagonism toward Freemasonry, published and distributed as a leaflet in 1698.**

TO ALL GODL₁ PEOPLE,
in the Citie of

LONDON.

HAving thought it needful to warn you of the Mischiefs and Evils practised in the Sight of God by those called Freed Masons, I say take Care left their Ceremonies and secret Swearings take hold of you; and be wary that none cause you to err from Godliness. For this devilish Sect of Men are Meeters in secret which swear against all without their Following. They are the Anti Christ which was to come leading Men from Fear of God. For how should Men meet in secret Places and with secret Signs taking Care that none observe them to do the Work of God; are not these the Ways of Evil-doers?

Knowing how that God observeth privilly them that It in Darkness they shall be smitten and the Secrets of their Hearts layed bare. Mingle not among this corrupt People lest you be found so at the World's Conflagration.

Set forth as a Warning to this Christian Generation by
M. Winter, and Printed by R. Sare at Gray's
Inn-gate, in Holbourn.
1698.

with Judaism, seeking world domination. Although completely without foundation, it would appear that dictators perceive Freemasonry as having the same aims as themselves and therefore a threat to be dealt with accordingly.

In Russia the Craft was revived in 1908 after being closed down by Czar Alexander I in 1822, but it did not last long and went out of existence again in 1922 under the Bolsheviks.

In 1925 Mussolini passed an anti-Masonic law in Italy, and Masonry was suppressed in Portugal in 1931.

Following Hitler's rise to power, Freemasonry in Germany ceased in 1935 when the Grand Lodge was dissolved. In *Mein Kampf* Hitler makes it quite clear that Freemasonry is the means through which Judaism wishes to achieve world domination.

Franco proscribed Freemasonry in Spain in 1941. In Rumania it was banned in 1948 and in Hungary in 1950. Sukarno banned it in Indonesia in the 1960s and it was proscribed in Pakistan in 1972. The Ayatollah Khomeini ended Freemasonry in Iran in 1979.

What is clear is that dictators at either end of the spectrum, whether communist or fascist, perceive Freemasonry as a threat to be dealt with ruthlessly. The one certainty is that all dictators have a limited shelf-life and eventually democracy returns and along with it Freemasonry.

Exposures of Freemasonry

There has always been considerable public interest and fascination about the various Masonic ceremonies. It is also true that right from the formal inception of Freemasonry in this country in 1717 the so-called secrets of Freemasonry have been the subject of what is known in Masonic circles as 'Exposures'. At a time when there were no officially printed rituals, these were bought in great numbers by Masons themselves so that they could in fact learn their ritual from them.

Bearing in mind that the first Grand Lodge was formed in 1717, it did not take long for the first Exposures to appear – the *Flying Post* in April 1723 (commonly referred to as *A Mason's Examination*) and *The Post Boy* of December 1723, the so called 'Sham Exposure'. Sham because it is thought that it was written by a Mason to mislead readers. Other Exposures followed including:

1723 The *Flying Post* Exposure
1723 The *Post Boy* Exposure
1724 *The Whole Institution of Masonry*
1724 *The Grand Mystery of Free-Masons Discover'd*
1730 *Masonry Dissected* by Samuel Prichard
1760 *Three Distinct Knocks*
1762 *Jachin and Boaz*
1802 Finch's *Masonic Treatise*
1826 *Morgan's Freemasonry Exposed and Explained*
1831 *Manual of Freemasonry* by Richard Carlile

Recent exposures have included: James Dewar, *The Unlocked Secret*, 1966; Stephen Knight, *The Brotherhood*, 1984 and Martin Short, *Inside the Brotherhood*, 1998.

The Internet is now a source of a choice of exposures and it is possible to download all the different Masonic ritual and ceremonies for most of the various Orders of Freemasonry – so much for the Secrecy of Freemasonry!

The one thing that can be said is that whilst over the years Exposures have come and gone, Freemasonry does not appear to have been adversely affected as a consequence.

Family History and Freemasonry

Research into family history has experienced a remarkable growth in the recent past. In that regard, knowing or wanting to know if a relative or ancestor was a Freemason is of some interest. Fortunately, the Library at Grand Lodge can help. If a lodge name or number is known, the enquiry service is provided free of charge. Where there is no lodge name or number then a fee is charged, but there is a reduction if the enquiry comes from a member of a lodge belonging to the United Grand Lodge of England. The information provided is usually fairly basic and normally gives the age, address, occupation and date of joining the lodge. Information about individual members is based on the Annual Return of members, compiled by individual lodges and sent to Grand Lodge. The earliest such Returns date from about 1768. Further information regarding family history and genealogical information can be found online or by contacting the Library and Museum of Freemasonry, Freemasons' Hall, 60 Great Queen Street, London WC2B 5AZ.

Famous Freemasons

This list of famous Freemasons from England and the United States is far from exhaustive and much more detailed lists may be found through the Internet.

Politicians
Edmund Burke, George Canning, Lord Randolph Churchill, Sir Winston Churchill, Cecil Rhodes.

Churchmen
Sir Israel Brodie, Geoffrey Fisher, Archbishop of Canterbury.

Scientists
Sir Alexander Fleming, Dr Edward Jenner, Sir Bernard Spilsbury.

Explorers
Sir Joseph Banks, Sir Richard Burton, Capt. Robert Falcon Scott RN, Sir Ernest Shackleton.

Actors
David Garrick, Edward Gibbon, Sir Henry Irving, Edmund Kean, Alexander Pope, Peter Sellers, Richard Brinsley Sheridan, Sir Donald Wolfit.

Authors
Robbie Burns, Sir Arthur Conan Doyle, Sir William S. Gilbert, Rudyard Kipling, Sir Walter Scott, Anthony Trollope, Oscar Wilde.

Artists
William Hogarth, Sir John Soane, John Zoffany.

Musicians
Thomas Arne, Sir Arthur Sullivan, Samuel Wesley.

Armed Services
Field Marshal Sir Claude Auchinleck, Field Marshal Earl Alexander of Tunis, Field Marshal Earl Roberts of Kandahar, Field Marshal Earl Kitchener of Khartoum, Field Marshal Sir John French Earl of Ypres, Field Marshal Earl Haig, Admiral Earl Jellicoe, General Sir Francis Wingate.

Entertainers
David Nixon, Cyril Fletcher, Geraldo, Sir Harry Lauder, Alfred Marks, Edmundo Ross, Tommy Trinder.

Sportsmen
Harold Abrahams, Sir Donald Campbell, Malcolm Campbell, Leslie Compton, 'Jack' Dempsey, Sir Leonard Hutton, Sir Clive Lloyd, Jackie Milburn, Sir Alec Rose, Len Shackleton, Jock Stein, Herbert Sutcliffe, Sir Thomas Lipton.

American Presidents
George Washington, James Monroe, Andrew Jackson, James Polk, James Garfield, James Buchanan, Andrew Johnson, William McKinley, Theodore Roosevelt, Howard Taft, Warren Harding, Franklin Roosevelt, Harry Truman, Gerald Ford.

American Frontiersmen and Revolutionaries
Kit Carson, Buffalo Bill Cody, Davey Crockett, Sam Houston, Benjamin Franklin, Paul Revere.

First recorded Freemason
In England the earliest reference to a Masonic Initiation is that of Elias Ashmole, dated 16 October 1646, who states in his diary that at:

> *4.30 p.m. I was made a Free Mason at Warrington in Lancashire, with.*
> *Col. Henry Mainwaring at Kerincham in Cheshire.*

The next reference in his diary relating to Masonry is not until 10 and 11 March 1682. On 10 March:

> *About 5H:p.m. I rec^d a Summons to appear at a Lodge to be held next*
> *day at Masons Hall London.*

Whilst on the 11th the entry reads:

> *Accordingly I went, & about Noone were admitted into the fellowship of*
> *Free Masons, Sr Willam Wilson Knight, Capt. Rich: Bortwick, Mr Will:*
> *Woodman, Mr Wm Grey, Mr Samuell Taylour & Mr William Wise.*
> * I was the Senior Fellow among them (it being 35 years since I*
> *was admitted). There were present beside my selfe the Fellows after*
> *named. Mr Tho: Wise Mr of the Masons Company this present yeare.*
> *Mr Thomas Shorthose, Mr Thomas Shadbolt, Wainsford Esqr, Mr Nich:*
> *Young, Mr John Shorthose, Mr William Hamon, Mr John Thompson, &*
> *Mr Will: Stanton.*
> * Wee all dyned at the Half Moone Tavern in Cheapside, at a Noble*
> *Dinner prepaired at the charge of the New-accepted Masons.*

His other claim to fame is that the collection of curiosities he gave to the University of Oxford in 1677 became what we know today as the Ashmolean Museum.

Fraternal Organisations
Fraternal organisations are more than just social organisations: the difference being that in the former members freely associate as equals for a mutually beneficial purpose. Examples from the past include City Guilds or Livery Companies, which were set up for the benefit of their members at a time when there was no welfare state

or health care. As with Freemasonry, the spread of state welfare has almost negated the original purpose associated with fraternal organizations – that of self-help. Nearly all have adapted their *raison d'être* from being solely self-help organizations to assisting others in need as well.

Modern-day examples operating in this country include:

The Independent Order of Odd Fellows, which dates from the 1700s and the *Royal Antediluvian Order of Buffaloes*, founded in 1822.

Membership of the *Knights of Saint Columba*, founded in 1919, is restricted to male Catholics in good standing, who must vow to 'defend their country, their families and their faith.'

Rotary International, founded in 1905, whose motto is 'Service above self', raises millions of pounds annually throughout the world which is spent on polio, education and other humanitarian issues.

Round Table claims to be the largest voluntary organization for young men in the world. Young being defined as below 45. It used to be 40 – but recruitment is a problem for all fraternal organizations these days. In the past those reaching the maximum age were eligible to join the '41 Club' – presumably in time it will become the '46 Club'.

There are many other fraternal organizations based in England and overseas that could be listed here but anyone interested in finding out more can easily do so through the Internet.

Freemasonry a religion?

Whilst Freemasonry has always been associated with teaching and encouraging morality, it has never been or considered itself a religion, a substitute for religion, or an alternative to religion. Freemasonry fails to meet any of the tests of what can be said to constitute a religion. Indeed, one of the great strengths of Freemasonry is that men of different faiths can meet in fellowship and harmony without any compromise of their religious beliefs. Since its earliest days, discussion of religion and politics have been prohibited in Lodge meetings.

Freemasonry and Charity

There are five main Masonic Charities – the four Craft Charities: The Grand Charity, The Royal Masonic Benevolent Institution, The Royal Masonic Trust for Girls and Boys and the Masonic Samaritan Fund; in addition one of the other Orders of Freemasonry – the Mark – has its own charity, known as the Mark Benevolent Fund, which celebrates its centenary in 2018.

One very important distinction between Freemasons and other worthy organisations such as Rotary International, the Lions or Round Table is that all monies collected, whether ultimately used for Masonic or non-Masonic charities, comes from the pockets of the members and not the general public.

It is still true today that if a Freemason, or one of his dependants, falls on hard times there are a number of Masonic Charities that will be able to assist. These include the Freemasons' Grand Charity, which provides assistance in the case of individual hardship. The Royal Masonic Trust for Girls and Boys aims to relieve poverty and advance the education of children of a Masonic family – to qualify for support a family must have suffered a distress which has resulted in financial hardship. The Royal Masonic Benevolent Institution has been caring for older Freemasons and their dependants for over one hundred and sixty years, and operates seventeen residential care homes across England and Wales; whilst the Masonic Samaritan Fund provides grants to those who have an identified health or care need and, faced with a long wait for treatment, care or support, are unable to afford their own private care. The Mark Benevolent Fund provides assistance to Mark Master Masons and their dependents in the case of individual need.

One common feature of all five Charities is that at their inception the concept was very much one of self-help, and to qualify for financial assistance one either had to be a Freemason or the dependant of a Freemason. In time, many of the original charitable purposes as they appertained to Freemasons and their dependants have changed dramatically with the introduction of a comprehensive welfare system and national health service. The self-help element is still there to assist those Freemasons who fall through the welfare safety-net, but significantly three of the Masonic Charities (the Grand Charity, Royal Masonic Trust for Girls and Boys and the Mark benevolent Fund) not only provide assistance in the case of individual hardship but also make extensive donations to non-Masonic charities.

Grand Charity

Every Freemason is automatically a member of the Freemasons' Grand Charity and his annual subscription includes a compulsory element (currently £17.00), which goes to the Charity.

The grants made by the Grand Charity fall into three main categories:

Masonic Relief Grants – providing financial assistance for Freemasons and their families who are experiencing hardship.

Grants to Charities – Support for the important work of national charities of all sizes, in medical research, support for vulnerable people, youth opportunities, hospice services, air ambulance services and disaster relief worldwide.

Other Masonic Charities – When justifiable needs arise, the Grand Charity will support the work of the other Masonic Charities.

In 2012, £5.1 million was approved in financial grants to help individuals in need, assisting over 2,000 people. Over 100 charities received a share of £1.7 million; 239 hospices received a total of £600,000; and 22 air rescue charities received a share of £192,000 – making a grand total of £7,757,758. Since 1981 the Grand Charity has donated over £50 million to national charities.

Royal Masonic Benevolent Institution (RMBI)
The RMBI provides sheltered accommodation, residential and nursing care in homes for older Freemasons and their dependants. There are 17 RMBI Homes, nearly 1,000 residents, 671 female residents and 317 male residents. Their average age is 88 years old and the average age on admission into an RMBI care home is 86. There are more than 466 residents over 90 years old and 23 residents over 100. In 2012 some 124 residents were admitted. Sadly, one third of the residents die each year.

Royal Masonic Trust for Girls and Boys (RMTGB)
In 1788 the Chevalier Bartholomew Ruspini and the Duchess of Cumberland founded a school for the daughters of distressed Masons, *The Royal Cumberland Freemasons' School for Female Objects*. A similar provision for boys was established in 1798.

Over the next two hundred years the Girls' Institution and the Boys' Institution grew larger and helped ever-increasing numbers of Masonic children at their schools and from time to time the schools relocated to larger premises. By the 1970s fewer and fewer beneficiaries were being sent to the Masonic schools and even more were receiving support whilst living at home. Eventually, the Boys' School at Bushey was sold and The Royal Masonic School for Girls at Rickmansworth is now an independent school for girls operating in the private sector.

1986 saw the amalgamation of the two former Institutions to form the Masonic Trust for Girls and Boys, which in May 2003 became the Royal Masonic Trust for Girls and Boys, and whose mission statement is currently 'To relieve poverty and advance the education of children of a Masonic family and, when funds permit, support other children in need.'

The Trust continues to help children and young people, using a variety of different funds and projects; however its main role is to assist the children of Masonic families who have experienced a distress that has led to financial hardship. In recent years, further schemes have been established to assist non-Masonic initiatives such as *TalentAid*, which helps to support children and young people who are exceptionally gifted in music, sport or the performing arts. The scheme was established in response to the growing awareness that some families were making huge financial sacrifices, or were simply unable to support their child's career ambitions in these fields. Since the scheme was established, over £3m in *TalentAid* grants have been awarded to over 250 young people whose exceptional talent often represents their best career prospect. The Choral Bursary scheme currently supports choristers at cathedrals across England and Wales. Smaller schemes such as *Stepping Stones* are pleased to receive applications from charities registered in England and Wales that are working to significantly improve life outcomes for young people from disadvantaged backgrounds. The RMTGB also has a number of subsidiary funds that are able to support charities like *Lifelites* – the only charity in the UK that provides cutting-edge computer technology for children and young people in children's hospices.

The Masonic Samaritan Fund

The Masonic Samaritan Fund is a charity funded by Freemasons and their families. It provides grants to eligible beneficiaries who have an identified health or care need and, faced with a long wait for treatment, care or support, are unable to afford their own private care.

The Mark Benevolent Fund (MBF)

The Mark Benevolent Fund came into existence in 1868 on the suggestion of the then Grand Master, the Reverend Canon George Raymond Portal. His views on charity were far more progressive and radical than the general thinking of the times. He believed it necessary for the Mark Degree to have its own Benevolent Fund because he was certain that if charity was to be effective it had to be dispensed swiftly and without the bureaucratic formalities. It was an anathema to him for there to be any delay in providing assistance to those in need and the Grand Master's own Latin motto *Bis dat qui cito dat* – he gives twice who gives promptly – became the principal guideline of the Fund of Benevolence.

Today, the MBF administers to Mark Master Masons and their dependents in need by means of grants. In addition it makes considerable financial grants to a range of Masonic and non-Masonic charities.

Since the establishment of the fund in 1868 the following grants have been distributed:

Grants to Individual Petitioners	£5,479,218
Major Grants to Worthy Causes	£13,308,665
Grants to Worthy Causes	£2,144,163
TOTAL	**£ 20,932,046**

None of the Masonic Charities derive any income from outside funding such as the National Lottery. Each of the Charities has an Annual Festival hosted by one of the forty-four of the forty-seven different Masonic Provinces (Guernsey & Alderney, Jersey and London are not included). It means that each Masonic Province can expect to host a Charity Festival every eleven years. The money raised is a significant element of that Charity's income. One of the problems is that the amount raised is in direct proportion to the number of members in the Province and hence there will be significant differences on a year-by-year basis. The members of the Province involved are encouraged to support the appeal over a period of some five or more years, usually with targets being set for individual lodges. The appeal culminates in a celebratory event – the Festival – when the final total is announced. By way of example, in 2018 the Charities being supported by the respective Provinces and the targets where set are as follows:

Grand Charity	*Gloucestershire*	£2.8m
Royal Masonic Benevolent Institution (RMBI)	*Suffolk*	tbc
Royal Masonic Trust for Girls and Boys (RMTGB)	*Nottinghamshire*	£3m
Masonic Samaritan Fund (MSF)	*North and East Riding*	£2.3m
Mark Benevolent Fund (MBF)	*Lincolnshire*	tbc

As can be seen, not inconsiderable sums are raised, almost entirely from the pockets of the members within the particular Province. The expectation is that every member will contribute sufficient – £500 – over the five-year appeal period to qualify as a Festival Steward.

Considerable charitable donations are made not only by the five national Masonic Charities but also by individual lodges, who not only give to the national charities but also raise money to donate to local non-Masonic charities. Little, if anything, is reported in the national press of the contribution made by Masonic Charities – the local press is more generous in its coverage. Fortunately Freemasons do not give to charity to gain publicity but only to try and make the world that little bit better.

Freemasonry in Literature

There are many examples of Freemasonry featuring in literature. Amongst the most recent are the works of Dan Brown. In his novel of 2003, *The Da Vinci Code,* the purported links with Knights Templar, the Holy Grail, Rossyln Chapel and Freemasonry are stretched to breaking point; whilst in *The Lost Symbol* of 2009 he puts Freemasonry in a very positive light. The references to Freemasonry contained in the *The Lost Symbol* relate, not surprisingly, primarily to American rather than English Freemasonry. Whilst the Masonic elements have been distorted, embellished and indeed, in some cases, invented, there is little doubt that in order to do so it had to be extremely well researched. One must remember that the book is a fictional thriller, which requires a level of suspension of belief regarding almost every aspect contained within it to make it work. It will, no doubt, in due time be the basis of an equally excellent film.

Sir Arthur Conan Doyle was not a particularly active Freemason, but there are at least seven references to Freemasonry that can be found in his writings, for example from *The Adventure of the Red-headed League* (1891):

> *'Beyond the obvious facts that he has at some time done manual labour, that he takes snuff, that he is a Freemason, that he has been in China, and that he has done a considerable amount of writing lately, I can deduce nothing else.'*
>
> *'Well, the snuff, then, and the Freemasonry?'*
>
> *'I won't insult your intelligence by telling you how I read that, especially as, rather against the strict rules of your order, you use an arc-and-compass breastpin.'*

P.G. Wodehouse was another less than keen Mason, but his work contains numerous references relating to Freemasonry. In *Blandings Castle* (1935) Wodehouse writes that to persuade Lord Emsworth's prize pig, the Empress of Blandings, to hoist aboard the vast amounts of nourishment needed to maintain her prize-winning form, her minder must loudly call 'Pig-oo-o-o-ey'. He goes on to say that 'it is, to the pig world, what the Masonic grip is to the human'.

One very keen and enthusiastic Freemason and author was Rudyard Kipling. His poem *The Mother Lodge* is referred to elsewhere and his works include many Masonic references, not least in his short story *The Man Who would be King* (1907):

> *'I ask you, as a stranger going to the West,' he said with emphasis.*
>
> *'Where have you come from?' said I.*
>
> *'From the East,' said he, 'and I am hoping that you will give him the message on the Square for the sake of my Mother as well as your own.'*

Limitations of space and the nature of this book mean that this particular subject, which is worthy of a book in its own right, must be tantalisingly brief in the extreme.

Gloves

During lodge meetings Freemasons wear a pair of white gloves. Symbolically, everything that a Freemason does should be pure and spotless and hence by wearing gloves it means that everything he touches will be with 'clean' hands.

Goats in Freemasonry

The supposed association between goats and Freemasonry goes back a long way. The word 'supposed' is important because there is no evidence whatsoever linking the two and certainly no reference to it in any Masonic ritual. My best guess is that in the early years of Masonry it was alleged that Freemasons 'raised the devil' during Masonic meetings; the goat was often used as a representation of the devil; it was believed that 'riding the goat' was practised by witches and somehow the two aspects were inter-changed. Yet, even today, it is common enough for Masons prior to an Initiation to make a nervous Initiate even more nervous by making some casual reference relating to whether the goat 'has been properly tethered' or to its size or temperament.

A watercolour of the Goose and Gridiron, the meeting place of the first Grand Lodge, painted by B. Angel Roberts in 1892.

Grand Lodge

It is known that Masonic lodges were operating in England as early as 1646 but it was not until 24 June 1717 that four lodges – that met respectively at the Goose and Gridiron Ale-house in St Paul's Churchyard (now *Lodge of Antiquity No. 2*); the Crown Ale-house in Parker's Lane near Drury Lane; the Apple-Tree Tavern in Charles Street, Covent Garden (now *Lodge of Fortitude and Old Cumberland No. 12*); and the Rummer and Grapes Tavern in Channel Row, Westminster (now *Royal Somerset House and Inverness Lodge No. 4*) – held a meeting at the Goose and Gridiron to form the first or Premier Grand Lodge. They elected Mr Anthony Sayer, Gentleman – the Master of the Lodge that met at the Apple-Tree – as the first Grand Master.

On 17 July 1751, representatives of six lodges met at the Turk's Head Tavern in Greek Street, Soho, London and formed another Grand Lodge – the 'Most Ancient and Honourable Society of Free and Accepted Masons according to the Old Constitutions', which became commonly known as the 'Antients'.

The reasons for the development and establishment of the second Grand Lodge are interesting for a number of reasons. From lodge records and returns it is possible to draw up a list of the occupations of members of lodges at the time, these included: Gentleman, Victualler, Merchant, Mariner, Law, Tailor, Army, Carpenter, Doctor/Surgeon, Baker, Goldsmith/Silversmith. Whilst the list of occupations is far from complete, as indeed are the records themselves, they at least give a reasonable indication of the state of affairs at the time. The significant feature relates to a comparison of the social composition of the members of the lodges under the two Grand Lodges: the Law, Mariner, Army, Doctor/Surgeon Merchant and Gentleman feature significantly in the Premier Grand Lodge. Whilst in the Antients Grand Lodge Tailor, Carpenter and Baker predominate in similar proportions. Victualler and Goldsmith/Silversmith appear in both Grand Lodges in almost equal proportions.

Hogarth's 1738 engraving *Night* shows in the foreground the Master, slightly the worse for wear, being escorted home by the Tyler of the Lodge, which met in nearby Channel Row at the Rummer and Grapes Tavern. The Lodge was one of the four that formed the first Grand Lodge in 1717.

It would appear that artisans, many of Irish origin, found it difficult to be accepted as members of the Moderns Grand Lodge and hence set up their own lodges in the first instance and ultimately their own Grand Lodge.

Another factor that developed in time was that the members of the Antients considered the ritual and ceremonial that was practised by them was the benchmark and that the Moderns had introduced unacceptable innovations. In part this is as a result of the fact that the Antients were largely influenced by Irish Freemasonry, not least in terms of the Warrants under which Antient lodges operated, which were modelled on those issued to Irish lodges. The Antients considered themselves to be the protectors of pure original Freemasonry and as a consequence of which, the original or Premier Grand Lodge was disparaging called the 'Moderns'.

It is significant that the membership of the *Antients* was to a large extent composed of artisans, shopkeepers and the like; whereas the membership of the *Moderns* was composed essentially of 'gentlemen' and those from the upper ranks of society.

The two Grand Lodges eventually came together whilst Edward, Duke of Kent was Grand Master of the Antients and Augustus, Duke of Sussex, Grand Master of the Moderns to form the United Grand Lodge of England (UGLE) in December 1813. The Duke of Sussex was made the Grand Master, in which office he served until his death in 1843.

UGLE is still the governing body of Freemasonry in England, Wales and the Channel Islands. Its headquarters are at Freemasons' Hall, Great Queen Street, London WC2B 5AZ, where Grand Lodge has been based since 1775.

Grand Lodge meets four times a year on the second Wednesday in March, June, September and December. The meetings are known as the Quarterly Communications and it is when all the official business of Grand Lodge is transacted. Membership of Grand Lodge, and hence speaking and voting rights, are restricted to Worshipful Masters and Past Masters whilst they continue to be subscribing members of a lodge. In recent years the regulations have been amended to enable Master Masons to attend meetings of Grand Lodge. The Annual Investiture, which is followed by the Grand Festival, is held on the last Wednesday in April; it is at this meeting that the new Grand Officers of the year are appointed and invested.

Grand Lodge Certificate

Having taken his Third Degree every Mason, having been registered, receives a Certificate from Grand Lodge. It comes folded and is presented during a lodge meeting. The new Mason is informed during the presentation that it constitutes a Masonic Passport and should be taken with him when he visits another lodge to prove his membership. Certificates have been issued since 1756. The present design was adopted in 1819 and is known as the 'Pillars' Certificate, since the design is dominated by the three pillars of Freemasonry. The certificate bears the Arms of the Grand Master which alter with each change of Grand Master. The last major amendment to the overall design took place in 1965, when only English wording was used rather than both English and Latin as previously.

Grand Rank

Freemasonry is no different to many organisations in having a hierarchical structure. The pyramidal structure consists of: the lodge at the base, then the Province, with Grand Lodge at the pinnacle. If a Mason enjoys his Freemasonry and is keen to progress, he will in time become the Master of his lodge. If he continues to work

An example of the Grand Lodge Certificate – the equivalent of a Masonic Passport – that is presented to all Freemasons on completing their Third Degree.

within his lodge and the Province, he will after five years or so be eligible to be considered for appointment to Provincial Grand Rank. Provincial and indeed Grand Ranks mirror to a large extent those in the lodge. The principal officers in a lodge include (by way of example) the Senior and Junior Wardens and the Senior and Junior Deacons. At Provincial level these become the Provincial Grand Senior and Provincial Grand Junior Warden; the Provincial Grand Senior and Provincial Grand Junior Deacon. At Grand Lodge level they translate to Grand Senior and Grand Junior Warden and Grand Senior and Grand Junior Deacon.

There are more ranks in Grand Lodge and Provincial Grand Lodge because there are more functions to fulfil – hence there is for example a Grand Sword Bearer (whose duties are self-evident) and a Grand Registrar, whose duties include giving legal advice as and when necessary. There are some seventy-eight Grand Officers appointed each year. In a Province (or overseas in a District) the number of ranks available each year is determined by the size of the Province. The greater the number of members in the Province, the larger the number of ranks available. The smallest Province with less than 1,000 members will have a maximum of twenty-two whilst the largest with more than 9,000 may appoint up to seventy-five Provincial Grand Officers.

However, even in the smallest Province the number of so-called 'active ranks' that may be awarded will always far exceed the number of candidates eligible for consideration. The same principle applies for appointment to Grand Rank. It is a considerable achievement for any Freemason to attain Grand Rank – the number awarded each year is limited and a Province is only able to recommend one candidate for approximately every 1,250 members. Every year something in the order of 225 Freemasons are appointed to Grand Rank, of whom only 78 can receive active rank – that is, be a Grand Officer for one year. The solution to the conundrum is resolved by the majority of recipients being appointed to *Past* Grand Rank – with all the same privileges as the active Grand Officers of the year. At the end of their period in office, active Grand Officers become Past Grand Officers, so ultimately they all become Past Grand Officers. A better description for those appointed to Past Rank as opposed to active rank is perhaps the one used in France and some other continental countries, where Past Rank is actually called 'Honorary' Grand Rank. For the sake of completeness, it should be added that in addition to appointment to Grand Rank, after some ten years there is the possibility of being promoted. The promotions are also limited in number: approximately one promotion for every 2,500 members in a Province.

Great Architect of the Universe

There is an unequivocal requirement that all candidates for Freemasonry profess a belief in a Supreme Being. In this country, to all intents and purposes, that means a belief in God.

Other religions have different names and concepts of God, all of which are entirely acceptable as far as Freemasonry is concerned. What is not acceptable is atheism or non-belief.

Almost since its inception, and certainly since 1723, Masonic ritual has referred to the concept of God or a Supreme Being as the Great Architect of the Universe – GAOTU. Other references in the Ritual also include the allegorical names Supreme Governor of the Universe and Grand Geometrician of the Universe.

There is nothing whatsoever in any Craft Masonic ritual that any member of any religious belief would find either offensive or unacceptable. All lodges in this country have to have a copy of a Volume of the Sacred Law (VSL) open during the meeting. The choice of words is not accidental. Whilst in the majority of cases the VSL will be the Bible, there is no reason why it should not be one of the holy books belonging to one of the major religions such as the Koran, Torah, *Bhagavad Gita*, *Ramayana*, *Veda* and *Avesta*. If a candidate for Freemasonry is not a Christian, then most lodges will make every effort to ensure that he takes his Masonic Obligation on the holy book of his religion.

Higher Degrees of Freemasonry and the Thirty-Third Degree – 33°

One sometimes hears the phrase 'He is a Thirty-Third Degree Freemason'. The implication being that he is in some way at the top of the Masonic tree. To an extent that is true, but it is not quite the whole story. Most non-Masons when they refer to Freemasonry are by default talking about Craft Masonry. All Freemasons when they join Freemasonry come into a Craft lodge (in the USA referred to as a 'Blue' lodge because of the predominant colour of the regalia that is worn). In the Craft lodge a Freemason will take the first Three Degrees of Freemasonry and the majority – over 50 per cent – will be more than content and not take any further steps in extending their Masonic knowledge beyond the Craft. In this country there are three main branches of Masonry: the Craft, including the Royal Arch; the Mark and other Orders of Freemasonry administered from Mark Masons' Hall; and the Ancient and Accepted Rite, sometimes referred to as the Rose Croix. Masonry in England, beyond the Craft, has been described in terms of arriving at a railway station, where there are a number of platforms, each going to a different destination and each of these is the equivalent of one of the Orders of Masonry. One can pick and choose which train to go on, as many or as few as one has the inclination, time and finance to do so. In the USA there are basically only two platforms and two trains to choose from, with the journey being progressive through each of the Orders: the York Rite (equivalent to the Orders administered from Mark Masons' Hall) and the Ancient and Accepted Rite, which in the USA is known as the Scottish Rite. Much of Dan Brown's excellent book *The Lost Symbol* is partly based in the headquarters building of the Southern Scottish Rite in

Washington, DC. It is a first-class read, but you will not learn too much about Masonic ritual as a consequence – I believe the phrase that can be applied is 'poetic licence' – but that does not detract from either the book or Dan Brown's view of Freemasonry.

It is the Ancient and Accepted Rite (A&A) that practises the thirty-three degrees of Freemasonry. So as to avoid any possible confusion or conflict of interest, the Rite does not work the first Three Degrees – the degrees of Craft Masonry. It would take many years to complete all thirty-three degrees so in England only the 18°, the 30°, 31°, 32° and 33° are worked in full. The so-called Intermediate Degrees are conferred in name only, but each year one or two, depending on their length, are demonstrated. Most A&A Masons who successfully pass through the Chair can reasonably expect to receive the 30°; after that it is a matter of 'dead men's shoes'. The number of ranks available at 31° and 32° are very limited and hence it can take many years to achieve that level, if ever. The 33° is also very restricted and is usually only achieved if one becomes the head of a District of the Order, with the title of Inspector General 33°. In a sense therefore a Mason who accomplishes the thirty-third degree has reached the top of the Masonic tree but in no way does it make him in some way superior to the Mason who has chosen to limit his Masonic experience only to Craft Masonry.

It should be added that, in this country, to be able to join the Ancient and Accepted Rite one has to profess a belief in the Christian Trinitarian Faith: a criterion that has existed ever since the Order came to this country in 1845. The same restriction does not apply in most other countries throughout the world, where the Ritual worked is known as 'Universal' and open to Brethren of all faiths.

Influence of Freemasonry on language

There are a number of aspects of Freemasonry that have crept into everyday language over the years. Most notably:

A Past Master – someone skilled in a particular area of work or expertise.

To be blackballed – referring to the fact that every candidate for membership has to be duly elected. The traditional method is by placing a white ball – if in favour – or a black ball – if against – in a ballot box. Lodge bylaws vary but anything between one and three blackballs are sufficient to prevent the candidate gaining membership.

To be given the third degree – means a close or intense interrogation. The phrase arises directly from the ritual of the Third Degree.

Acting on the square or *on the level* – dealing with somebody in a straight forward and honest manner.

Initiation Ceremony

There are a considerable number of organisations that as part of their joining procedure require a candidate to go through some form of initiation ceremony. Freemasonry is by the far the best known initiatory organisation but others include fraternal organisations such as the Knights of Columbus, fraternities and sororities in the USA, trade unions, the military, gangs and tribal communities.

Freemasonry has been described as 'a peculiar system of morality veiled in allegory and illustrated by symbols'.

Taken at face value, what takes place at a lodge meeting is a series of ceremonies. Craft Masonry consists of three stages or Degrees, with the Candidate progressing from the First to the Second and Third. In Masonic terminology these are known as the Initiation, Fellowcraft and Master Masons' Degrees respectively.

It is true to say that all Masonic ceremonies consist of several key elements. The ritual or ceremonial of the Three Degrees in Freemasonry are progressive and follow a similar pattern. A different Opening/Closing procedure for each individual Degree, which ensures that those present are properly qualified to participate in that part of the ceremony. An introduction, where it is ascertained and made clear to those present that whilst the Candidate is not yet a member of that particular Degree he has the necessary attributes and qualities to enable him to receive the appropriate secrets to become qualified.

The blessing of God is invoked on the proceedings. An Obligation or oath is taken by the Candidate, in which he promises not to divulge the secrets that are about to be entrusted to him. Having taken the Obligation, the Candidate is entrusted with the secrets associated with the particular Degree. These usually consist of a sign, a grip or token of recognition and a secret word or series of words.

The sign is only given in a Lodge Room as part of a ceremony, as indeed are the secret words associated with each Degree. In so far as the signs are concerned, they would look distinctly odd if given in a public place, rather than in a Lodge Room.

The secret word (or rather words, as there are three, one for each of the Three Degrees) are just that. As with the three signs, it is difficult to imagine a situation where a Mason goes up to someone and whispers in his ear one of the three secret words. In the lodge the secret word is used in a symbolic way, simply to confirm that those there are entitled to be present during that part of the ceremony.

The grip or token of recognition is 'the secret handshake' of the title of the book. This token or handshake is supposed, in theory, to enable one Mason to recognise another by day as well as by night. The word 'supposed' is important. Whilst a limp handshake is usually a sure indication that the person concerned is not a Freemason, a firm handshake is no certainty that he is. Each of the Three Degrees requires pressure to be applied to a different part of the other's hand. Easier said than done. During the course of a lodge meeting great care is taken to ensure that the thumb is placed in exactly the right position – with clinical precision if the Director of Ceremonies has anything to do with it. Out of the Lodge Room it is not easy to reproduce with any degree of certainty. It may be difficult to believe, but it is extremely unlikely that a Freemason would recognise a fellow Freemason simply through the means of a handshake!

The majority of the ceremony is carried out by the Master of the lodge and is done from memory. In some lodges, Past Masters will share part of the ceremony, to help spread the workload. This book is not meant to be an exposé or indeed Exposure of Masonic ritual. Those reading this book who might one day aspire to become Masons should wait until they are initiated to find out what happens – otherwise it is a similar experience to being told the finale of a film or play prior to seeing it. Anybody else can discover the full details either by buying the ritual book from a Masonic supplier or online – or indeed finding the ritual in its entirety on the Internet.

International Freemasonry

Freemasonry is active throughout the free world. In theory any group of Freemasons can set themselves up as a Grand Lodge, but in practice, to be accepted by the rest of the legitimate Masonic world, it needs to be formally recognised and for that to happen there are series of agreed criteria that have to be satisfied, not least that the Grand Lodge concerned is accepted as being 'Regular'. One of the major reasons that 'Recognition' is so important is that it enables inter-visiting to take place between the members of the respective Grand Lodges.

The rules relating to the 'Recognition' and the 'Regularity' of Grand Lodges were adopted as long ago as 1929. The Grand Lodge of England has eight basic principles that have to be satisfied before another Grand Lodge can be recognised and which may be summarised as follows:

1. Be regular in its origin (no less than three properly constituted lodges deciding to form themselves into a Grand Lodge)
2. Be truly independent and self-governing
3. Continue to uphold certain Masonic 'Landmarks', which are:

   a) The Brethren must believe in a Supreme Being
   b) Obligations must be taken on or in full view of the VSL (Bible)
   c) The three Great Lights of Freemasonry (VSL, Square and Compasses) must be displayed when the Lodge is open
   d) Discussion of religion and politics in lodge is prohibited
   e) Membership must be male, and have nothing to do with mixed or women's lodges.

On that basis and according to the latest information available on their website, the following 194 Grand Lodges are recognised by the United Grand Lodge of England:

Grand Lodge of Ireland, Grand Lodge of Scotland;

Grand Lodge of Albania, Grand Lodge of Andorra, Grand Lodge of Armenia, Grand Lodge of Austria, Regular Grand Lodge of Belgium, Grand Lodge of Bosnia and Herzegovina, United Grand Lodge of Bulgaria, Grand Lodge of Croatia, Grand Lodge of Cyprus, Grand Lodge of Czech Republic, Grand Lodge of Denmark, Grand Lodge of Estonia, Grand Lodge of Finland, United Grand Lodges of Germany, Grand Lodge of Greece, Symbolic Grand Lodge of Hungary, The Icelandic Order of Freemasons – Grand Lodge of Iceland, Regular Grand Lodge of Italy, Grand Lodge of Latvia, Grand Lodge of Lithuania, Grand Lodge of Luxembourg, Grand Lodge of Macedonia, Sovereign Grand Lodge of Malta, Grand Lodge of Moldova, National Regular Grand Lodge of the Principality of Monaco, The Grand Lodge of Montenegro, Grand East of The Netherlands, The Norwegian Order of Freemasons – Grand Lodge of Norway, National Grand Lodge of Poland, Legal Grand Lodge of Portugal, National Grand Lodge of Romania, Grand Lodge of Russia, Grand Lodge of the Most Serene Republic of San Marino, Regular Grand Lodge of Serbia, Grand Lodge of Slovakia, Grand Lodge of Slovenia, Grand Lodge of Spain, The Swedish Order of Freemasons – Grand Lodge of Sweden, Grand Lodge Alpina of Switzerland, Grand Lodge of Turkey, Grand Lodge of Ukraine;

Grand Lodge of Benin, Grand Lodge of Burkina Faso, Grand Lodge of Cameroon, Grand Lodge of Congo, Grand Lodge of Gabon, Grand Lodge of Ghana, National Grand Lodge of Guinea, Grand Lodge of Ivory Coast, Grand Lodge of the Republic of Liberia, National Grand Lodge of Madagascar, National Grand Lodge of Mali, Grand Lodge of Mauritius, The Regular Grand Lodge of the Kingdom of Morocco, Grand Lodge of Senegal, Grand Lodge of South Africa, Grande Loge Nationale Togolaise;

Grand Lodge of China, Grand Lodge of India, Grand Lodge of the State of Israel, Grand Lodge of Japan; Grand Lodge of the Philippines;

Grand Lodge of New Zealand, Grand Lodge of New South Wales and Australian Capital Territory, United Grand Lodge of Queensland, Grand Lodge of South Australia and the Northern Territory, Grand Lodge of Tasmania, Grand Lodge of Victoria, Grand Lodge of Western Australia;

Grand Lodge of Alberta, Grand Lodge of British Columbia and Yukon, Grand Lodge of Canada in the Province of Ontario, Prince Hall Grand Lodge of Ontario, Grand Lodge of Manitoba, Grand Lodge of New Brunswick, Grand Lodge of Newfoundland and Labrador, Grand Lodge of Nova Scotia, Grand Lodge of Prince Edward Island, Grand Lodge of Quebec, Grand Lodge of Saskatchewan;

Grand Lodge of Alabama, Grand Lodge of Alaska, Prince Hall Grand Lodge of Alaska, Grand Lodge of Arizona, Prince Hall Grand Lodge of Arizona, Grand Lodge of Arkansas, Grand Lodge of California, Prince Hall Grand Lodge of California, Grand Lodge of Colorado, Prince Hall Grand Lodge of Colorado, Grand Lodge of Connecticut, Prince Hall Grand Lodge of Connecticut, Grand Lodge of Delaware, Prince Hall Grand Lodge of Delaware, Grand Lodge of the District of Columbia [Washington DC], Prince Hall Grand Lodge of the District of Columbia [Washington DC], Grand Lodge of Florida, Grand Lodge of Georgia, Grand Lodge of Hawaii, Prince Hall Grand Lodge of Hawaii, Grand Lodge of Idaho, Grand Lodge of Illinois, Prince Hall Grand Lodge of the State of Illinois, Grand Lodge of Indiana, Prince Hall Grand Lodge of Indiana, Grand Lodge of Iowa, Prince Hall Grand Lodge of Iowa, Grand Lodge of Kansas, Prince Hall Grand Lodge of Kansas, Grand Lodge of Kentucky, Grand Lodge of Louisiana, Grand Lodge of Maine, Grand Lodge of Maryland, Prince Hall Grand Lodge of Maryland, Grand Lodge of Massachusetts, Prince Hall Grand Lodge of Massachusetts, Grand Lodge of Michigan, Prince Hall Grand Lodge of Michigan, Grand Lodge of Minnesota, Prince Hall Grand Lodge, Jurisdiction of Minnesota, Grand Lodge of Mississippi, Grand Lodge of Missouri, Prince Hall Grand Lodge of Missouri, Grand Lodge of Montana, Grand Lodge of Nebraska, Prince Hall Grand Lodge of Nebraska, Grand Lodge of Nevada, Prince Hall Grand Lodge of Nevada, Grand Lodge of New Hampshire, Grand Lodge of New Jersey, Prince Hall Grand Lodge of New Jersey, Grand Lodge of New Mexico, Prince Hall Grand Lodge of New Mexico, Grand Lodge of the State of New York, Prince Hall Grand Lodge of New York, Grand Lodge of North Carolina, The Prince Hall Grand Lodge of North Carolina, Grand Lodge of North Dakota, Grand Lodge of Ohio, Prince Hall Grand Lodge of Ohio, Grand Lodge of Oklahoma, Grand Lodge of Oregon, Prince Hall Grand Lodge of Oregon, Grand Lodge of Pennsylvania, Prince Hall Grand Lodge of Pennsylvania, Grand Lodge of Rhode Island, Prince Hall Grand Lodge of Rhode Island, Grand Lodge of South Carolina, Grand Lodge of South Dakota, Grand Lodge of Tennessee, Grand Lodge of Texas, Prince Hall Grand Lodge of Texas & Jurisdictions, Grand Lodge of Utah, Grand Lodge of Vermont, Grand Lodge of Virginia, Prince Hall Grand Lodge of Virginia, Grand Lodge of Washington, Prince Hall Grand Lodge of Washington, Grand Lodge of West Virginia, Grand Lodge of Wisconsin, Prince Hall Grand Lodge of Wisconsin, Grand Lodge of Wyoming;

Grand Lodge of Argentina, Grand Lodge of Bolivia, Grand Orient of Brazil, Grand Lodge of the State of Mato Grosso Do Sul, Grand Lodge of the State of Rio De Janeiro, Grand Lodge of the State of São Paulo, Grand Lodge of the State of Espírito Santo, Grand Lodge of Chile, Grand Lodge of Colombia at Barranquilla, Grand Lodge Oriental of Colombia 'Francisco de Paula Santander', Grand Lodge of Colombia at Bogota, Grand Lodge of Colombia at Cali, Grand Lodge of Colombia at Cartagena, Grand Lodge of Los Andes, Grand Lodge of Ecuador, Symbolic Grand Lodge of Paraguay, Grand Lodge of Peru, Grand Lodge of Uruguay, Grand Lodge of the Republic of Venezuela;

Grand Lodge of Costa Rica, Grand Lodge of Cuscatlan of El Salvador, Grand Lodge of Guatemala, York Grand Lodge of Mexico, Grand Lodge of Panama;

Prince Hall Grand Lodge of the Commonwealth of the Bahamas, Prince Hall Grand Lodge of The Caribbean and Jurisdiction, Grand Lodge of Cuba, Grand Lodge of the Dominican Republic, Grand Orient of Haiti 1824, Grand Lodge of Puerto Rico.

This means that, having first checked with UGLE and made the necessary arrangements, it is possible for an English Freemason to visit lodges all round the world. The need to check is important, not least because situations can and do change. For a number of reasons the Grande Loge Nationale Française (GLNF) has had recognition withdrawn and so English Freemasons are currently unable to visit or become members of that Constitution; in time one hopes the situation can be resolved and fraternal relations can be resumed.

King Solomon's Temple

The Three Degrees of Craft ritual are based on certain aspects relating to the building of King Solomon's Temple in Jerusalem. Whilst some elements on which it is based may be found in the Bible, others are contained in the Apocrypha. The basic story centres on Hiram Abiff, the principal architect of the building. Everyday at noon Hiram climbs the steps into the unfinished Sanctum Sanctorum to work on the designs for the building and to pray. One day he is accosted by three Fellow Craft Freemasons – Jubela, Jubelum and Jubelo – who attempt to extract from him the secrets of a Master Mason. Being an honourable man, Hiram refuses to give them and is killed for his troubles. The three ruffians hastily bury Hiram in a shallow grave, marked with an acacia plant. Next day King Solomon discovers that Hiram is missing; a search party is organised and finds the grave identified by the acacia plant; the ruffians are captured and punished. King Solomon and Hiram, King of Tyre travel to the grave and, despite the decomposed state of the

An engraving of King Solomon's Temple. The events surrounding
the building of this play a significant element in Masonic ceremonies.

body, manage to raise it and arrange for it to be buried in the Temple near the
Sanctum Sanctorum. Such is the so-called Hiramic legend, intertwined with which
is the symbolism associated with the building of the Temple that forms the basis of
today's Masonic ritual.

The first time that the legend of King Solomon's Temple appears in Masonic
literature is in the *Constitutions* of the Order published in 1738. The first set of
Constitutions was drafted in 1723 but do not contain any information relating to
the legend. It is thought that the inclusion in 1738 was to add a certain element of
gravitas to the relatively new Order of Freemasonry by suggesting that the roots of
Freemasonry went all the way back to King Solomon.

Knights Templar and Freemasonry

The original Knights Templar were a group of knights formed to protect Christian
pilgrims in the Holy Land after Jerusalem was captured in 1099. The original
name was the Order of Poor Fellow-Soldiers of Christ and the Temple of Solomon.
This started to evolve into a chivalric order of warrior-monks after 1129, when
members began taking monastic vows of poverty, chastity and obedience. The
distinctive uniform worn by the Templars was a white tunic bearing an eight-

81

pointed red cross. The Order continued to develop, especially after 1139, when Innocent II exempted them from lay and ecclesiastical jurisdiction – to the extent that in 1177, during the Battle of Montgisard, some 500 Templars helped defeat Saladin's army. The Templars continued to grow in wealth and influence but tensions increased between the Templars, the Church and the various states where they operated, especially France. To the extent that on Friday 13 March 1307 King Philip of France, under duress from Pope Clement V, ordered the arrest of the Templar's Grand Master, Jacques de Molay. The Templars were charged with numerous offences, not least heresy, idolatry, obscene practices, homosexuality, corruption and fraud. Under torture, many of those accused confessed to these charges. King Philip put considerable pressure on Pope Clement, who finally agreed to disband the Order in 1312, citing the public scandal that had been generated by the confessions. Notwithstanding that, many later retracted their confessions and a considerable number were burned at the stake, including Jacques de Molay in Paris on 18 March 1314. In September 2001 a document known as the 'Chinon Parchment' and dated 17-20 August 1308 was discovered in the Secret Archives of the Vatican. A record of the Templar trials, it shows that Clement absolved the Templars of all heresies in 1308 before formally disbanding the Order in 1312.

Following the disbandment of the Order, rumours began to circulate regarding the final resting place of the various relics allegedly in the possession of the Templars, including the Holy Grail, the Ark of the Covenant, the head of Saint Euphemia of Chalcedon, a piece of the True Cross and the Shroud of Turin, to name but a few.

One particular legend is that after the dissolution of the Order some surviving members sought refuge and brought the Holy Grail to Scotland. Rosslyn Chapel, near Edinburgh, was built some one hundred and fifty years after the disbandment and contains carvings of many Masonic and Templar symbols, such as a carving that appears to show a figure being prepared to be a candidate for Freemasonry and another showing the seal of the Knights Templar – 'two riders on one horse'. This and other features have led a number of writers to attempt to suggest that modern Freemasonry is directly descended from the original Knights Templar.

Notwithstanding this absolutely fascinating but entirely implausible theory, the Masonic Order of Knights Templar makes its appearance in the late eighteenth century.

Baron Von Hund claimed that he was made a member of a reconstituted non-Masonic Templars Order in 1743. In 1751 he produced a Masonic Ritual known as the Order of Strict Observance, which has evolved today predominantly in continental Europe into an Order of Masonic Knights Templar known as the Knights Beneficent of the Holy City.

In England the first Grand Conclave of Knights Templar was formed in 1791 with Thomas Dunckerley as Grand Master. The Order still flourishes today as 'The United Religious, Military and Masonic Orders of the Temple and of St John of Jerusalem, Palestine, Rhodes and Malta'.

Ladies' Nights

The Ladies' Night, which still prevails in many Masonic lodges, is an annual dinner or dinner-dance, at which the Master presides but it his wife, or lady, that is the guest of honour. In many ways it is seen as a thank-you and recognition of the fact that the men could not carry out their Freemasonry without the support of their ladies. There is no doubt that in many instances it used to be the social highlight of the year and in some instances continues to be so, particularly outside London.

In London the situation has materially altered, for no better reason than cost. A Ladies' Night in London is almost prohibitively expensive, not just with the high cost of dining, room hire and a live band, but also because of the drink-driving laws that necessitate a taxi home or an overnight stay in a hotel. This is the main reason why a number of lodges started to have Ladies' Weekends (rather than Ladies' Nights), in places such as Bournemouth or Eastbourne or even further afield, as the overall cost was very similar and better value for money.

A whole industry has developed around the concept of Ladies' Nights, even generating books on the subject. The planning for a Ladies' Night can take on the same proportions as that for a wedding, and is taken equally seriously.

Dinner-dances are very passé these days and not the type of social event that is likely to appeal to a younger generation. Having said that, Freemasons are by their very nature conservative and hence the Ladies' Night or Weekend is here to stay for some time yet.

Law

Although it is often alleged that Freemasons have sought more lenient sentences when found guilty in court by making secret Masonic signs to the judge, there is no evidence to suggest or even prove that any such action was successful. Indeed the only example I have come across where an attempt has been made to influence a judge in this way is as far back as 1912.

Frederick Seddon had been found guilty of the murder of his lodger, Miss Eliza Mary Barrow. On being asked by the Clerk of the Court if he had anything to say as to why the sentence of death should not be passed against him, Seddon made the sign of either the First Degree or the Sign of Grief and Distress from the Third Degree (accounts vary) to the presiding judge Sir Thomas Townsend Bucknill, and as a brother Mason asked the judge in the name of 'The Great Architect of the Universe' to overturn the jury's guilty verdict.

Seddon had been initiated into Stanley Lodge No. 1325 in Liverpool in 1901 and in 1905 was the Founder of a Lodge at Bourne End in Buckinghamshire, Stephens Lodge No. 3089. By 1906 he had resigned from both Lodges. The trial judge, Sir Thomas Bucknill, had been initiated in 1873 into Lodge of Good Report No. 136 and at the time of the trial was the Provincial Grand Master for Surrey.

Mr Justice Bucknill is reported as saying, with some emotion:

> *It is not for me to harrow your feelings – try to make peace with your Maker. We both belong to the same Brotherhood, and though that can have no influence with me, this is painful beyond words to have to say what I am saying, but our Brotherhood does not encourage crime, it condemns it.*

He then pronounced the sentence of death: Seddon was hanged in Pentonville Prison on 18 April 1912.

Lewis

In building terminology a 'lewis' is a form of hoist used to lift large stones. In Masonry it refers to the son of a Freemason.

Lodge meeting – what happens?

In essence a lodge night is composed of three elements: the meeting itself, pre-dinner drinks and dinner. A normal lodge meeting consists of some five parts: an opening ceremony, some day-to-day business, a degree ceremony, a further element of Lodge business together with any communications from the Provincial or Grand Lodge, and a closing ceremony. All in all, a lodge meeting normally lasts some two hours. Pre-dinner drinks and dinner then follow. It is not unusual for the key members of a lodge to hold a rehearsal of the Degree ceremony, either before the formal meeting starts or more likely in the week previously. Although practice varies, most lodge meetings take place in the evening, starting at about 5.00 p.m. or 6.00 p.m. and finishing after dinner at about 10.00 p.m.

Lodges as private clubs

To all intents and purposes Masonic lodges are independent private clubs. To become a member, as with most other clubs, one needs to be proposed and seconded by two existing members.

Just as with any other private club, a lodge has a Chairman, save that he is known as the Worshipful Master. As might reasonably be expected, every lodge has a complement of regular officers who hold office for one or more years. These include a Secretary and a Treasurer who effectively manage the day-to-day affairs of the lodge.

Lodges of Instruction

In order to ensure that the ceremony is carried out to best effect many lodges hold a weekly Lodge of Instruction (LOI). The meeting is basically a simplified lodge meeting – the prime purpose being to rehearse the various Masonic ceremonies. After the LOI the members will often stay for a drink. The LOI may take place in the same building in which the lodge normally meets, but it would not be unusual for the LOI to take place in a private room in a local hostelry.

In addition to a regular Lodge of Instruction, or in some instances a Circle of Instruction, that has a similar but less formal structure, many lodges hold a rehearsal for the officers of the lodge – an Officers' Night – a week or so before the actual lodge meeting.

Masonic Collectables, Artefacts, Memorabilia and Ephemera

Given the fact that Freemasonry has been operating in this country since before 1717, it is not surprising that over the years it has generated many collectable items such as jewellery, silverware, glassware and pottery. This is in addition to such things

A number of countries are proud to be associated with Freemasonry and this is reflected in the postage stamps that are issued from time to time.

as medals or jewels. Masonic books are another area that appeals to the Masonic collector; as is the collection of Masonic postage stamps and postcards.

A number of associated organisations have grown up to foster interest in these areas, such as the *Jewels of the Craft* (JOTC) that was formed in 1990 by a number of Freemasons with a common interest in Masonic jewels. The Masonic Philatelic Club serves a similar purpose for Masonic stamp and postcard collectors.

It simply goes to show that there is more to Freemasonry than just attending Masonic meetings and learning ritual.

Masonic Fire

At the conclusion of a Masonic dinner there will be a number of formal toasts that are usually concluded with Masonic Fire.

The main toasts are those to the Queen, the Grand Master, the Provincial Grand Master and the Master. Other toasts may include those to the Grand Officers, Provincial Grand Officers, the Candidate and the Visitors.

Some of the toasts will receive either no formal response or perhaps a short response; others such as those to the Master or Visitors may result in a more lengthy reply. Regrettably not all Freemasons are natural after-dinner speakers and Freemasons (being usually good mannered) are too polite to advise them accordingly.

Masonic Fire is believed to have been copied from the practice followed at military dinners, and is said to replicate the firing of guns in salute. It derives from the time when Masonic lodges were held round a table in a tavern. After the toast had been given, the glass was drained of its contents and banged on the table, in appreciation of what had been heard and to show that the glass was empty and ready to be re-filled. In time, no doubt because of sustained breakages, special firing glasses began to be made – too small to drink out of but with a heavy bulbous bottom that meant that they could be safely banged on the table without fear of breaking – whilst the wine continued to be served in traditional drinking glasses. As not all lodges have firing glasses, the action and noise is simulated in most lodges by clapping the hands to a particular rhythm.

Masonic Funerals

Until 1962 when the practice was banned by Grand Lodge it was not unusual for Masons to have a Masonic Funeral. The practice came to the fore in the Victorian era. In essence a Lodge of Mourning was opened in the local Lodge Room and then 'called off' or adjourned. The Master, accompanied by the Brethren, then processed to the house of the deceased wearing full Masonic regalia and from there accompanied the coffin to the church and cemetery. It was not unusual for the deceased Brother's regalia to be placed on the coffin. Once the coffin was lowered into the grave, the Masons present threw a sprig of acacia onto the coffin, as well as the more traditional handful of soil. After the funeral the members processed back to the Lodge Room so that the lodge could be properly closed.

Some fifty years on, it seems strange to think that it was ever considered appropriate, but customs alter with the passage of time, as was stated in the report to the Board of General Purposes:

> ...*the intrusion into the proceedings both of the Master of his Lodge and also of the former Brethren of the deceased, had become unwelcome to his widow, to the clergy and to the non-Masonic mourners.*

The report went on to say that there should be:

> ...*no active participation by Masons, as such, in any part of the burial service or cremation of a brother, and that there be no Masonic prayers, readings, or exhortations either then or at the graveside subsequent to the interment, since the final obsequies of any human being, Mason or not, are complete in themselves and do not call in the case of a Freemason for any additional ministrations.*

Masonic Publications

Masonic publishing has been in existence for as long as Freemasonry. One of the first references to an article about Freemasonry is found in the *The Tatler*, a short-lived English publication founded by Richard Steele in 1709, in the issue of Tuesday, 7 June 1709. In an anonymous letter addressed to Isaac Bickerstaff, Richard Steele's nom de plume, we find the following:

> ...*do assume the Name of Pretty fellows; nay, and even get new Names, as you very well hint. Some of them I have heard calling to one another...by the Names of, Betty, Nelly, and so forth. You see them accost each other with effeminate Airs: They have their Signs and Tokens like Free-Masons...*

Books

In 1912 August Wolfsteig published a Masonic Bibliography consisting of three volumes and containing well over 43,000 entries, recognizing 8 classes with some 174 sub-divisions. That however is a topic for another day.

Masonic Year Books and Pocket Companions

Other early publications were the pocket companions. Although at first sight this may seem surprising, on reflection it should be no surprise at all: the pocket companions were useful in that they contained such things as the history of Freemasonry and the Charges and Regulations, together with collections of songs and poetry. Most usefully though they contained a list of lodges, their times of meeting and meeting places. Hence, these were very handy if you wished to visit other lodges. Examples of early pocket companions include: *Smith's Pocket Companion* (1735) and *Scott's Pocket Companion* (1754).

Constitutions and Regulations; Masonic jurisprudence

The first official publication of Grand Lodge was the so-called 'Anderson' *Constitutions*, published in 1723. A common aspect of many official publications is the time lag involved before publication. So it should not be a surprise that the first set of regulations for the fledging Grand Lodge followed some six years after its formation in 1717.

As an interesting aside, Benjamin Franklin, who initially wrote some less than flattering pieces about Masonry, saw the error of his ways and was initiated in 1731. In 1734, whilst he was Master of his lodge, he published in Philadelphia the first Masonic book in America: an American version of the 'Anderson' *Constitutions*.

In 1738 a revised edition of Anderson's *Constitutions* was published; and following the formation of the 'Antients' Grand Lodge in 1751 Laurence Dermott wrote their Constitutions, named enigmatically *Ahiman Rezon* and published in 1753. Note the time lag again.

Masonic literature: poetry, music, essays, and orations

Examples of early books include:

> *Brotherly Love Recommended*, Chas. Brockwell, 1750, Boston, USA
> *Light and Truth of Masonry*, Thomas Dunkerley, 1757

Music and poetry feature very largely in early Masonic books, as it was the custom to include music and songs in Masonic proceedings. Both Anderson's *Constitutions* of 1723 and *Ahiman Rezon* of 1751 include extensive sections containing both Masonic poetry and music.

Magazines

The first Masonic periodical was *Der Freymäurer*, a weekly magazine published in Leipzig in 1738.

The first English Masonic periodical, the *Freemasons' Magazine*, or *General and Complete Library*, appeared in June 1793.

The *Masonic Record* ran for fifty years until 1970 and the *Freemasons' Magazine* managed a short run of only fifteen years up to 1963. In many ways the successor

The frontispiece to the first *Constitutions* of the Free-Masons of 1723 showing John Montague, 2nd Duke of Montagu presenting the Roll of Constitutions and the compasses to his successor as Grand Master, Philip, Duke of Wharton.

to both magazines was the *Masonic Square*, launched in 1975; the title of which became *The Square* in 1997.

Freemasonry Today is the house journal for the United Grand Lodge of England. Starting as an independent magazine in 1998, it combined with the previous house journal of UGLE, *Masonic Quarterly* (*MQ*), in 2007.

Newspapers
The Freemason had a colossal run from 1869-1951; eighty-two years as a weekly newspaper. *The Freemason's Chronicle*, which was also a weekly newspaper, co-existed with *The Freemason* for almost the same period, 1875-1957.

Masonic Rituals
The United Grand Lodge of England has never sanctioned or published any official ritual. Indeed, the printing of the ritual was initially opposed by Grand Lodge.

The link between Exposures and rituals is best demonstrated by Carlile's *Manual of Freemasonry* which first appeared in *The Republican* in 1825 and was printed in book form as *An Exposure of Freemasonry or a Mason's printed Ritual with an Introductory Keystone to the Royal Arch of Freemasonry* in 1831.

Some handwritten rituals existed prior to 1813. The earliest ritual book, that included the Three Degrees, questions before Passing and Raising and the Installation of the Master and officers was published by George Claret in 1838. After Claret's death in 1850 his widow continued to sell the book until 1870. Further editions were published, the last in 1873.

Claret's *Ritual* was superseded in 1871 by a book entitled *The Perfect Ceremonies of Craft Masonry*. The publisher was John Hogg, writing under the pseudonym of A. Lewis, presumably because of concern about possible opposition from Grand Lodge. The book was a resounding success and it continued in print until 1969. The publisher eventually became A. Lewis (Masonic Publishers) Limited. In 1973 the company was taken over by Ian Allan Publishing and became known as Lewis Masonic.

Masonic rituals can be bought through Masonic suppliers or online, and regrettably all Masonic rituals are now freely available to be downloaded from certain overseas sites on the Internet – so much for secrecy!

Meeting on the level
In Masonic jargon 'one meets on the level' whilst in the lodge, but social order is restored again once the meeting has ended. Two examples that best exemplify the principle relate to two incidents arising in the United States: one relating to Theodore Roosevelt and the other to an incident which occurred at Gettysburg during the Civil War.

Theodore Roosevelt

President Theodore Roosevelt is one of fourteen Presidents of the USA to have been a Freemason. He was initiated in January 1901 into a lodge in Oyster Bay, New York. At a White House lunch, the question of Masonry came up and it transpired that every man present was a Mason. The President remarked that one of the aspects of Freemasonry that appealed to him was the fact that it brought men together from very different stations of life. 'Do you know,' said the President, 'that the Master of my Lodge is just a working man, a gardener for one of my neighbours in Oyster Bay; but when I visit Matinecock Lodge he is my boss, and I must stand up when he orders me, and sit down when he tells me, and not speak unless he allows me.' W. M. James Duthie was the gardener referred to by the President: a Scot who was Master of Matinecock Lodge for three years during President Roosevelt's first administration in 1902-1904. He was the Senior Warden of the Lodge when Roosevelt was raised. The lunchtime conversation was witnessed by the Revd Alexander G. Russell, pastor of the Presbyterian Church at Oyster Bay, who was present at the lunch and published the anecdote in a memoire dated 1919.

The Bingham-Hancock Incident at the Battle of Gettysburg

This incident is commemorated by a monument on the battlefield at Gettysburg, presented by the Grand Lodge of Pennsylvania in 1993 and dedicated as a memorial to the Freemasons of the Union and the Confederacy. As the inscriptions on either side of the monument state:

> *Their unique bonds of friendship enabled them to remain, a brotherhood undivided, even as they fought as a divided nation, faithfully supporting the respective governments under which they lived.*

and

> *Union General Winfield Scott Hancock and Confederate General Lewis Addison Armistead were personal friends and members of the Masonic Fraternity.*

> *Although they had served and fought side by side in the United States Army prior to the Civil war, Armistead refused to raise his sword against his fellow Southerners and joined the Confederate Army in 1861.*

> *Both Hancock and Armistead fought heroically in the previous twenty-seven months of the war. They were destined to meet at Gettysburg.*

During Pickett's Charge, Armistead led his men gallantly, penetrating Hancock's line. Ironically, when Armistead was mortally wounded, Hancock was also wounded.

Depicted in the sculpture is Union Captain Henry Bingham, a Mason and staff assistant to General Hancock, himself wounded rendering aid to the fallen Confederate General. Armistead is shown handing his watch and personal effects to be taken to his friend, Union General Hancock.

Hancock survived the war and died in 1886. Armistead died at Gettysburg, July 5 1863. Captain Bingham attained the rank of general and later served 32 years in the United States House of Representatives. He was known as the 'Father of the House'.

The values of Masonry include honesty, integrity and commitment. The incident described above shows that, even at times of considerable strife such as war, it is still possible to act honourably and with a considerable degree of humanity – on the level.

Meeting Places in cities, towns and villages

It is possible to group lodges into three very broad categories: those that meet in London, in large urban conurbations, and those that meet in small provincial towns and villages. London is in a unique situation not mirrored anywhere else in the world. There are some 1,400 lodges and 40,000 Freemasons meeting within five miles of the centre of London: a large number of them at Freemasons' Hall in Great Queen Street – the headquarters of English Freemasonry. The greater majority of those Freemasons will either work or have previously worked in London and live out in the suburbs. It means that the members of the lodge meet together but at the end of the evening disperse to all parts of the metropolis. The situation is mirrored in other cities such as Manchester, Liverpool and Nottingham, amongst many others.

One of the heydays of Masonry was the period immediately prior to the Second World War and it was at this time that a large number of purpose-built and imposing Masonic Halls were built, including Freemasons' Hall in London, which in addition to the spectacular Grand Temple has twenty-one purpose-built lodge rooms. It is a Grade II* listed building, open to the public and one of the finest examples of Art Deco in the country. The Halls in the three cities mentioned above were also built at about the same time and boast similar facilities, albeit on a smaller scale.

In the suburbs lodges tend to meet in purpose-built or adapted centres. For example in Middlesex there are five Masonic Centres. The one in Twickenham was previously a hotel and was converted for Masonic use back in the 1950s. Some one hundred different units meet there, which is approximately the same number as meet in the whole of Nottinghamshire. In so far as provincial towns and villages are concerned, not unexpectedly, the number of lodges is very much smaller. By way of example, a town such as Newark-on-Trent, with a population of approximately 26,000, has one meeting place which is a converted, large suburban villa which is home to five lodges. Most of the members will live and work in the locality and even in a large town such as Newark may well come across each other in other aspects of community life.

A smaller town may well only have one lodge meeting there, either in its own premises or perhaps in a local hotel. A favourite conversion for a meeting place is that from a church or chapel. Given the internal height of such buildings it is relatively easy to put in a new floor, so that the Lodge Room can be accommodated on the first floor with the dining room on the ground floor, together with space for a bar and changing facilities. A small extension at the back is usually sufficient to house the kitchen, and any garden left over makes a useful car park.

A lodge based in a village or rural area may not have the resources or a suitable site for its own Masonic meeting place. It is not unusual for a village hall to be used for that purpose, the main room being used as the Lodge Room. After the meeting the Lodge Room is broken down by the members and converted into a dining room. Whilst this is being done the other members and visitors to the lodge can enjoy a few drinks – the number of drinks often being governed by the length of time it takes to convert the room from one use to the other! In such circumstances it is not unusual for the wives of the members to be responsible for preparing the food, which would then be served by the Stewards of the lodge. At the other end of the spectrum, lodges meeting in London are just as likely to dine somewhere like the Connaught Rooms, immediately next door to Freemasons' Hall, a nearby pub, restaurant or hotel or even one of the London Clubs – the ambience and the cost varying accordingly. In the Provinces the meal following the meeting may cost in the order of £20.00 including wine whilst in London the cost is likely to be in the order of £50.00, rising to £75.00 or more at a five-star hotel or restaurant or a London Club.

Mother Lodge

The Lodge into which a Freemason is initiated is known as his Mother Lodge, even though he may well become a Joining Member of other lodges in the future.

The importance of the Mother Lodge to a Freemason and the relationship of Freemasonry with ethnicity, religion and occupation are best summed up in Rudyard Kipling's poem:

The Mother Lodge

There was Rundle, Station Master,
An' Beazeley of the Rail,
An' 'Ackman, Commissariat,
An' Donkin' o' the Jail;
An' Blake, Conductor-Sargent,
Our Master twice was 'e,
With 'im that kept the Europe-shop,
Old Framjee Eduljee.

Outside – "Sergeant! Sir! Salute! Salaam!"
Inside – "Brother", an' it doesn't do no 'arm.
We met upon the Level an' we parted on the Square,
An' I was Junior Deacon in my Mother-Lodge out there!

We'd Bola Nath, Accountant,
An' Saul the Aden Jew,
An' Din Mohammed, draughtsman
Of the Survey Office too;
There was Babu Chuckerbutty,
An' Amir Singh the Sikh,
An' Castro from the fittin'-sheds,
The Roman Catholick!

We 'and't good regalia,
An' our Lodge was old an' bare,
But we knew the Ancient Landmarks,
An' we kep' 'em to a hair;
An' lookin' on it backwards
It often strikes me thus,
There ain't such things as infidels,
Excep', per'aps, it's us.

For monthly, after Labour,
We'd all sit down and smoke
(We dursn't give no banquits,
Lest a Brother's caste were broke),
An' man on man got talkin'
Religion an' the rest,
An' every man comparin'

Of the God 'e knew the best.

So man on man got talkin',
An' not a Brother stirred
Till mornin' waked the parrots
An' that dam' brain-fever-bird;
We'd say 'twas 'ighly curious,
An' we'd all ride 'ome to bed,
With Mo'ammed, God, an' Shiva
Changin' pickets in our 'ead.

Full oft on Guv'ment service
This rovin' foot 'ath pressed,
An' bore fraternal greetin's
To the Lodges east an' west,
Accordin' as commanded
From Kohat to Singapore,
But I wish that I might see them
In my Mother-Lodge once more!

I wish that I might see them,
My Brethren black an' brown,
With the trichies smellin' pleasant
An' the hog-darn[1] passin' down;
An' the old khansamah[2] snorin'
On the bottle-khana[3] floor,
Like a Master in good standing
With my Mother-Lodge once more!

Outside – "Sergeant! Sir! Salute! Salaam!"
Inside – "Brother", an' it doesn't do no 'arm.
We met upon the Level an' we parted on the Square,
An' I was Junior Deacon in my Mother-Lodge out there!

Rudyard Kipling (1865-1936)

[1] cigar-lighter
[2] butler
[3] pantry

The poem *Mother Lodge* first appeared in the *The Seven Seas* in 1896.

Music and Freemasonry

A number of prominent musicians have written music specifically for Masonic occasions.

The most famous is no doubt Wolfgang Amadeus **Mozart** (1756-1791) who not only composed music specifically to be used in Masonic ceremonies but also the opera *The Magic Flute,* which is full of Masonic overtones.

Jean Sibelius (1865-1957) became a member of Suomi Lodge No. 1 in 1922, a Lodge which was established in 1922 after Finland gained its independence from Russia. Not surprisingly, he became the Lodge organist in 1922, and agreed to compose some *'original, genuinely Finnish music for the lodge'.* His *Masonic Ritual Music,* or *Musique religieuse,* opus 113, of nine movements, received its first complete performance on 12 January 1927. Sibelius added two further movements – 'Ode to Fraternity' and 'Hymn' – some twenty years later.

Sir William Schwenck **Gilbert** (1836-1911) and Sir Arthur Seymour **Sullivan** (1842-1900) were both enthusiastic Freemasons. Their comic operas are well known, but it is less well known that their final work together, *The Grand Duke* (first performed in March 1896), contained an amusing parody of Freemasonry. The first act contains an exchange relating to a secret sign:

> *LUDWIG:*
> *That has nothing to do with it. Know ye not that in alluding to our conspiracy without having first given and received the secret sign, you are violating a fundamental principle of our Association?*

> *LUDWIG SINGS:*
> *By the mystic regulation*
> *Of our dark Association,*
> *Ere you open conversation*
> *With another kindred soul,*
> *You must eat a sausage-roll!*

> *ALL SING:*
> *You must eat a sausage-roll!*

> *LUDWIG :*
> *If, in turn, he eats another,*
> *That's a sign that he's a brother -*
> *Each may fully trust the other.*
> *It is quaint and it is droll,*
> *But it's bilious on the whole.*

> *ALL SING:*
> *Very bilious on the whole.*

John Philip Sousa (1854-1932) is best known for his American military and processional patriotic marches, including 'The Liberty Bell'; 'Semper Fidelis' and 'The Stars and Stripes Forever'. His Masonic compositions include the march 'Nobles of the Mystic Shrine', dedicated to the Ancient Arabic Order of the Nobles of the Mystic Shrine – otherwise known as the Shriners.

Organisation of Freemasonry

The United Grand Lodge of England currently has over a quarter of a million members meeting in more than 8,000 lodges, which are grouped as follows:

Lodges meeting in London (an area generally within a 10-mile radius of Freemasons' Hall) are administered by the Metropolitan Grand Lodge of London, headed by the Metropolitan Grand Master.

Lodges meeting outside London, and within England, Wales, the Isle of Man and the Channel Islands, are grouped into forty-seven Provinces, whose boundaries often correspond to those of the old counties, with each headed by a Provincial Grand Master.

Lodges that meet outside England, Wales, the Isle of Man and the Channel Islands are grouped into thirty-three Districts, with each headed by a District Grand Master and five Groups (i.e. currently too small to make up a District), with each headed by a Grand Inspector; and there are twelve lodges abroad which are directly administered by Freemasons' Hall.

Origin and History of Freemasonry

The origin and history of Freemasonry is not straightforward and still the subject of much debate amongst Masonic scholars. The provenance of Freemasonry, as it at present exists in this country, can be traced back to 24 June 1717, when at a meeting held at the Goose and Gridiron Ale-house in St Paul's Churchyard, the first or Premier Grand Lodge was formed and elected Mr Anthony Sayer as the first Grand Master. It is known that Masonic lodges were operating in England as early as 1646, but records are fragmentary and incomplete.

There are two parallel histories of Freemasonry: one part mythology and part fiction and the other (as far as possible) factual.

In so far as the mythological history of Freemasonry is concerned, there are three main strands.

The first publication, known as Anderson's *Constitutions*, appeared in 1723, six years after the formation of the Grand Lodge in 1717. This was followed in 1738 with a new edition that for the first time included something of the supposed origin and history of Freemasonry. The kindest thing that can be said about the historical content is that it is rather fanciful in its attempt to link the foundation of Freemasonry back to the stonemasons associated with the building of King Solomon's Temple in Jerusalem. It was an early example of public relations – or more accurately 'spin' – at work and was no doubt aimed at raising both the credibility and profile of Freemasonry.

Another similar strand relates to the Knights Templar and their supposed link with Freemasonry. This particular legend is essentially that after the dissolution of the Knights Templar in 1312 some surviving members of the Order sought refuge in Scotland. Rosslyn Chapel near Edinburgh was built some 150 years after the disbandment of the Order and contains carvings of many Masonic and Templar symbols, including one that appears to show the seal of the Knights Templar – 'two riders on one horse'. This and other features have led a number of writers to attempt to suggest that modern Freemasonry is directly descended from the original Knights Templar.

A third strand suggests that Freemasonry evolved directly from medieval stonemasons, involved in, amongst other things, the building of the early cathedrals and castles. The stonemasons were transient craftsmen who moved from site to site and lived alongside the building under construction, in temporary lean-to structures known as lodges. Stonemasons were highly skilled and one of the earliest trades to form themselves into a guild early in the twelfth century. The main reasons for this included the provision of financial assistance in times of illness or difficulty in obtaining work, and, just as important, payment for funeral arrangements. As the guilds developed they began to regulate their trade activities, including wages, and to control entry into the craft through a system of apprenticeships. The guilds also devised a system of rituals that included the taking of oaths to protect the secrets or 'mysteries' of their craft; and a series of 'Charges' that laid down the responsibilities of each class within the organisation, such as apprentice and master mason. An apprentice would traditionally be indentured to a master mason for a period for seven years.

The missing link from all three different strands is how the transition from 'operative' stonemason to 'non-operative', 'speculative', 'gentleman', or 'accepted' Freemason – all of which are virtually synonymous – actually came about. Put crudely – how did the workmen living in rough, temporary accommodation on a building site with minimal facilities translate into a prestigious dining club for gentlemen?

The third strand of stonemasons' guilds offers the best starting point for a plausible explanation of the origin of Freemasonry. We can then move from those guilds to look at the Livery Companies and Trade Guilds which are today found primarily in London but also in a number of provincial cities such as Bristol, Sheffield, Glasgow and Edinburgh.

In England, evidence is very sparse and not helped by the destruction of the records of the Masons' Company in London. The Company has been in existence since at least the fourteenth century; its Hall, which had been leased from 1463, was purchased by

An example of an early design of a Lodge summons – still in use today.
Note the original use of the word 'affectionately'.

the Company in 1563. Unfortunately the Hall and most of the Company records were destroyed in the Great Fire of 1666, although the Hall was subsequently rebuilt.

One therefore has to turn to Scotland, where good written records still exist and where, in 1583, William Schaw was appointed Master of the Works by King James VI of Scotland. His responsibilities as Master of the Works grew and he eventually took charge not only of the masons responsible for all royal buildings but also of all masons in Scotland. In that capacity he issued two codes of conduct: the *Schaw Statutes* of 1598 and 1599. The statutes laid down regulations for all 'masons' through a system of lodges. The lodges referred not to sites located at a particular building, but to all masons working in a certain town or district. These lodges became organised and institutionalised, with elected officials under the direction of a warden. *Schaw's Statutes* defined two grades of masons: entered apprentice and fellow craft (also known as a master). In due course the fellow craft class was divided to form the separate grades of fellow craft and master mason.

During the early part of the seventeenth century some Scottish lodges started to admit 'non-operative', 'gentlemen' or 'accepted' masons, who wished to participate in the rituals and ceremonies that took place in lodges that were predominantly populated by 'operative' or working stonemasons. It is has to be appreciated that rituals involving the taking of oaths to protect the secrets of particular grades within an organisation are not peculiar to either 'speculative' lodges or indeed the guilds of other trades or professions. A practice incidentally that until at least the 1960s was still the case in some English Trade Unions.

'Non-operative', 'gentlemen', or 'accepted' Masons admitted to Scottish operative lodges paid a higher entrance fee and level of subscription than the operative masons. Prior to 1701 sixteen lodges have been identified in Scotland that admitted non-operative masons, the earliest six lodges going as far back as 1599. In time, it would appear that some lodges developed a dual role, with the operative or trade side being kept separate from the 'masonic' side. Eventually the transition from 'operative' to 'speculative' was concluded when the two different functions were totally split and the lodge worked as two separate entities, leading in due course to the formation of entirely separate and distinct 'speculative' lodges.

Many aspects of Freemasonry today mirror the organisation of the Livery Companies of London. Their original purpose has already been examined. With the passage of time Livery Companies have changed substantially. Today some Livery Companies, notably the Goldsmiths', Scriveners' and Apothecaries', are still actively involved in the organisation of their respective professions. The greater majority, whilst endeavouring to retain some form of link with their historical trade origins – for example Bowyers', Basketmakers' and Fanmakers' – are primarily involved in supporting charitable initiatives and social activities within the City of London.

In the City of London there are currently some 109 Livery Companies, each of which is usually governed by the Master, who is normally elected to hold office for one year. He is supported by two Wardens, although some Livery Companies, notably the Goldsmiths', are governed by a Prime Warden. All the various crafts and trades had their secrets, relating to their working practices – the 'mysteries'. These are still referred to when a Freeman takes an oath on admission into a Livery Company or (as often as not) in the Grace said prior to a livery dinner or banquet, such as that of the Clockmakers' Company:

> *For good food and good fellowship*
> *God's Holy name be praised*
> *And may He preserve the Church and Queen*
> *And ever prosper the Art and Mystery of Clockmaking*
> *Amen*

As has already been said, English records are sparse and incomplete. Reference has been made elsewhere to the Initiation of Elias Ashmole in 1646 at the house of a Col. Henry Mainwaring in Warrington. This indicates that speculative lodges were working in England at the time. There is a considerable gap in knowledge to be filled between 1646 and the formalisation of Freemasonry in England in 1717. The transition that Freemasonry has experienced has many similarities with that of the London Livery Companies and, whilst one cannot ignore the Scottish dimension, the connection between that and the situation in England has currently to remain 'not proven'.

Other Orders of Freemasonry

In this country there are three main branches of Freemasonry.

The first and main branch of Masonry is the Craft. Indeed, in England, you cannot join any other aspects of Masonry unless you are first a member of the Craft. The Headquarters are at Freemasons' Hall, in Great Queen Street, London; and since 1967 the Grand Master has been HRH The Duke of Kent.

Craft Masonry has a second element – the Holy Royal Arch Chapter or just Chapter: the headquarters are also in Great Queen Street, and the Grand Master, or more accurately First Grand Principal, is also HRH The Duke of Kent.

Unusually, this is one of very few countries in the world where the Craft and Chapter are inextricably linked. Elsewhere, including Scotland and Ireland, they are separate and distinct, with different Grand Masters and different administrations.

Some 50 per cent of Freemasons are content not to expand their knowledge or membership of Masonry beyond the Craft. The other 50 per cent join the Royal Arch Chapter or one of the other two branches of Freemasonry in addition to the Craft.

The second branch relates to those Degrees and Orders administered from Mark Masons' Hall. The largest of the Orders is the Mark, the Grand Master of which is HRH Prince Michael of Kent. The other Orders are: Royal Ark Mariner, Knights Templar, Allied Masonic Degrees, Order of the Secret Monitor, Red Cross of Constantine, Royal and Select Masters, Scarlet Cord and Knights Beneficent of the Holy City.

The third Branch is known as the Ancient and Accepted Rite or – more colloquially though not strictly accurately ' – the Rose Croix, with its headquarters in Duke Street, St James's, London. There are thirty-three degrees to be attained in this Order: the fact that only a very small minority achieve all these is explained further in the section on Higher Degrees.

P2

P2, or Propaganda Due to give it its full title, was an Italian Masonic Lodge under the Grand Orient of Italy. Its Warrant was withdrawn in 1976 but it continued as an underground, or rather underworld, 'lodge' until 1981. Mired in scandal, it was implicated in a number of Italian criminal activities, including the murder of banker Robert Calvi, who was found hanging under Blackfriars

The Grand Master of the Craft, HRH The Duke of Kent together with his brother, HRH Prince Michael of Kent, the Grand Master of the Grand Lodge of Mark Master Masons, in their respective regalia at the sesquicentenary celebrations of GLMMM in 2006.

Bridge in London. Needless to say, P2 had nothing to do with Freemasonry as it exists in this country but unfortunately it did nothing to enhance the reputation of Freemasonry worldwide, not least with those anxious to find fault with the organization.

Five and a half thousand members and their wives celebrating the sesquicentenary of the Grand Lodge of Mark Master Masons at the Royal Albert Hall in London in 2006.

Persecution of Freemasons

The most obvious example of the persecution of Freemasons was that undertaken by the Nazis during the Second World War. Very rarely, if ever, is it acknowledged that Freemasons were persecuted for their membership of the Craft and many perished in the Holocaust.

The Nazis made the distinction between Jews as a racial enemy of the German people and Freemasons as the ideological or political enemy.

One of the reasons why Freemasons are not identified as a separate group targeted by the Nazis is because they were inextricably linked with Judaism in the phrase 'Jews and Freemasons.' As often as not, Freemasons have not been specifically recognised as suffering during the Holocaust because they were considered as members of a sub-group. Hence a Jewish Freemason was a victim because he was a Jew, not because he was a Freemason. The one thing that can be said about the Nazis is that they were efficient in their record keeping. Hence Freemasons are listed as such and not, for example, Freemasons and Trade Unionists or Freemasons and Jews. However, efficient record keeping meant that dual membership was acknowledged and designated by a combination of signs. A Freemason would wear a Red Triangle (point down) and if he also happened to be a Jew the Red Triangle would be overlaid on a Yellow Triangle (point up) forming a six-pointed star. In a similar way a homosexual who was a Jew would have a Pink Triangle (point down) overlaid on a Yellow Triangle (point up) again forming a six-pointed star.

It is known that the Nazis had a comprehensive list of Freemasons in this country and there is little doubt that, had their invasion of Britain succeeded, Freemasons in this country would have suffered the same fate as their Brethren in continental Europe.

A series of anti-Masonic and anti-Semitic stamps issued by Serbia in 1942 to commemorate the Grand Anti-Masonic Exhibition held in Belgrade the previous year.

Police

In March 1997 the House of Commons Home Affairs Committee reported on the results of an investigation into Freemasonry in the Police and the Judiciary. Certain members of the Committee appeared to be convinced that Freemasons are members of some form of sinister secret society who unjustly exert unfair influence in promoting and defending other Freemasons. They seemed to believe that Freemasons are engaged in a conspiracy to hide wrongdoing by other Freemasons; apparently abetted by judges who exonerate criminals whom they recognise as fellow Freemasons from secret signs made from the dock. A non sequitur, given that Freemasons should, in theory, never appear in court. Some members of the Committee appeared equally convinced that policemen who are Freemasons fail to take appropriate action against other Freemasons who have committed crimes.

The Committee took evidence from a wide range of people, including the Lord Chancellor, the Magistrates' Association, the Association of Chief Police Officers, the Judiciary, the Bar Council, the Crown Prosecution Service and a number of individuals.

The long and short of it is that none of the organisations detailed above offered any evidence that Freemasonry caused any problems, or exercised any undue influence; nor had they any record of such issues arising.

Notwithstanding the lack of evidence, the committee agreed the following: 'We recommend that police officers, magistrates, judges and crown prosecutors should be required to register membership of any secret society and that the record should be publicly available.'

One cause of satisfaction, on my part, is that even given the openly anti-Masonic stance of some members of the Committee, they were not able to find any conclusive evidence of the adverse influence of Freemasonry in the Police and the Judiciary.

There followed in 1999 a second report by another Home Affairs Committee: this time on Freemasonry in Public Life.

The findings of that Committee, which started where the previous committee had left off, included the following:

> *We repeat the point made in the previous Report: there is a great deal of unjustified paranoia about Freemasonry, but Freemasons, with their obsessive secrecy, are partly to blame for this.*
>
> *…We are also aware that there is a widespread belief that improper Masonic influence does play a part in public life. Most of these allegations are impossible to prove. Where they can be carefully examined, they usually prove unfounded. It is clear, however, from some of the examples cited in this Report, and the previous Report, that there are cases where allegations of improper Masonic influence may well be justified.*

If it is *that* clear that there are cases '…where allegations of improper Masonic influence may well be justified' – all I will say is, why was not the opportunity taken to investigate them?

What *is* clear is that the various allegations made against Freemasons and the 'pernicious' influence of Freemasonry appear to be based on warped perception and not fact.

Prayers and Odes

Prayers are used in Masonic ceremonies at the Opening and Closing of each of the Three Degrees, and when the blessing of God is invoked on the proceedings during a ceremony. In some lodges it is the practice for an Opening and Closing Ode to be sung.

For example, the prayers in the First Degree and the Opening Ode are as follows:

Opening Ceremony – First Degree

> *The Lodge being duly formed, before I declare it open, let us invoke the assistance of the Great Architect of the Universe in all our*

undertakings; may our labours, thus begun in order, be conducted in peace, and closed in harmony.

Opening Ode

Hail! Eternal! by whose aid
All created things were made; Heaven and earth Thy vast design;
Hear us, Architect Divine!
May our work begun in Thee, Ever blest with order be;
And may we when labours cease,
Part in harmony and peace.
By Thy Glorious Majesty -
By the trust we place in Thee –
By the badge and mystic sign –
Hear us! Architect Divine!
So mote it be.

Prayer – First Degree

Vouchsafe Thine aid, Almighty Father and Supreme Governor of the Universe, to our present convention, and grant that this Candidate for Freemasonry may so dedicate and devote his life to Thy service as to become a true and faithful brother among us. Endue him with a competency of Thy divine wisdom, that, assisted by the secrets of our Masonic art, he may the better be enabled to unfold the beauties of true godliness, to the honour and glory of Thy Holy Name.

The concept of starting a meeting with prayer is not unique to Freemasonry. In this country Parliament starts each daily sitting with prayers, as do most local authority Council meetings. What is clear is that whilst this concept has until very recently been accepted as part of the fabric of our society, it is now being challenged more and more in the increasingly secular society in which we live.

Press

The relationship between the Press and Freemasonry is an interesting one. At the present time one can reasonably differentiate between the local press and the national press, which includes television and radio. In so far as the local press is concerned, Freemasonry does feature and usually in a positive light. More and more Masonic Centres hold 'Open Days' when members of the local community are invited to have a look round and find out a little more about Masonry. As often as not, these 'Open Days' are covered in the local press and, apart from the stereotypical headlines at the head of the piece such as 'Masonic Secrets Revealed', are generally sympathetic. Likewise lodges try and support local non-Masonic charities in their area and when a substantial cheque is handed over both the local lodge and the charity itself are pleased to receive some favourable publicity.

The situation with the national press is entirely different. You will very rarely, if ever, find a 'good news' story regarding Freemasonry. I recall being involved, a few years ago in 2006, with the sesquicentenary celebrations of the Grand Lodge of Mark Master Masons. The celebrations at the Royal Albert Hall were attended by the Grand Master, HRH Prince Michael of Kent, HRH The Duke of Kent, HRH Princess Michael of Kent, HRH The Duchess of Cornwall (in her capacity as the President of the National Osteoporosis Society) – not to mention five and a half thousand Freemasons and their wives. Grand Lodge marked the occasion by making a donation of £3 million, the largest single donation in the history of the Society. The National Osteoporosis Society could not have done more in terms of issuing press-releases and briefing notes to the national media. The result – not one column inch; not one mention on radio or television.

However, any hint of scandal or suggested scandal involving a Freemason will ensure full and lurid coverage.

This was not always the case. Until just after the Second World War Freemasonry featured prominently in both the local and national press. Reference was often made to the fact that a person was a Freemason in a positive rather than derogatory sense. In the local press detailed reports of Masonic meetings were a regular feature. The reasons for the change in relationship from respectability to suspicion are manifold, but there is little doubt that at present Freemasonry is viewed with mistrust by the national press, and there seems very little that Freemasonry, despite its best efforts, can do about it.

Prince Hall Freemasonry
In the United States the issues of slavery and subsequent widespread racial segregation resulted in Freemasonry developing along parallel, segregated lines.

Having been rejected by white lodges in Boston, Mass., in 1775, Prince Hall (his first name was Prince) and some other free black men were initiated into the travelling army Lodge No. 441 of the Irish Constitution. When the army left Boston in 1776, Prince Hall and his Brethren were given the authority to continue their Masonry as African Lodge No. 1. On 29 September 1784 the Premier or Moderns Grand Lodge of England issued a Warrant to this Lodge, now numbered African Lodge No. 459.

African Lodge contributed to the Grand Lodge Charity Fund until 1797 and was in correspondence with Grand Lodge until 1802, when communication ceased and contact between the two was lost. In 1797 African Lodge, with no authority from England, formed two Lodges: African Lodge No. 459B to meet at Philadelphia in Pennsylvania and Hiram Lodge (without a number) to meet at Providence, Rhode Island. At the formation of UGLE in 1813, the rolls of both the Moderns and Antients Grand Lodges were combined into one. African Lodge was omitted from the register, but not formally erased. What is now known as the Prince Hall Grand Lodge of Pennsylvania was formed in 1815. African Lodge was refused recognition by the Grand Lodge of

The Grand Master, HRH The Prince of Wales (later King Edward VII), laying the foundation stone of Truro Cathedral in 1889.

Massachusetts in 1827, and declared itself to be an independent Grand Lodge. After a number of attempts to form a National African Grand Lodge, the term 'Prince Hall Grand Lodge' was adopted in the 1840s.

All Prince Hall Grand Lodges are descended from what is now the Prince Hall Grand Lodge of Massachusetts and most of the States in the United States of America have a Prince Hall Grand Lodge. Until the latter part of the twentieth century the growth of Prince Hall Masonry was as a direct result of widespread racial segregation, which made it very difficult for an African-American to join a lodge outside the Prince Hall system. The lack of Recognition by the other State Grand Lodges made inter-visiting between the two impossible. It is open for any Grand Lodge to apply for Recognition, but in the ordinary course of events UGLE will only recognise one Grand Lodge in each geographical area or state. It will, however, in certain circumstances recognise a second Grand Lodge, providing that the first Grand Lodge to have been recognised does not have any objection.

As far back as 1994 UGLE resolved that, notwithstanding its unusual formation, the Prince Hall Grand Lodge of Massachusetts should be accepted as regular, and recognised. Since then UGLE has continued to grant Recognition to Prince Hall

Grand Lodges whenever possible, as the list detailed elsewhere amply illustrates. The history and development of Prince Hall Masonry in the United States of America is a reflection of the fact that Freemasonry mirrors the social mores of the society within which it is based. Fortunately considerable progress has been made in recent years and today, out of fifty-one US Grand Lodges, all except seven recognise their Prince Hall counterparts.

Public Processions and the public face of Freemasonry

From the early years of Freemasonry until the Second World War it was not uncommon for Freemasons to process in public wearing their regalia. The processions took place for a variety of reasons, including the laying of foundation stones of public buildings, attendance at church services and the annual Investiture and Festival of Grand Lodge.

However, the procession through the streets of London to the Grand Feast (Annual Meeting) ceased as long ago as 1747 when the Freemasons were satirised through so-

A parade in Welshpool to mark Queen Victoria's Diamond Jubilee in June 1897. Shown walking in procession here are officials of the Corporation and members of the town's Lodge.

called 'Mock Processions'. Although not quite the same thing, in the last few years Masons in regalia have formed part of the traditional Lord Mayor's Show in London.

It is not unusual for most Masonic Provinces to hold an annual service in the largest church in the Province, usually the cathedral, wearing full regalia.

Permission is rarely given these days by Grand Lodge for a public procession of Masons in regalia to take place. The last two occasions both took place in the north-east – in 2000 when the foundation stone of the re-sited Park Terrace Sunderland Masonic Hall was laid; and then in 2006 when the Grand Master, HRH The Duke of Kent, officially opened the Beamish Masonic Hall.

It was not always thus. In 1874 the memorial stone of the new Town Hall in Leicester was dedicated by the Deputy Provincial Grand Master, William Kelly and the full details were recorded in the local press.

Between 1875 and 1901 the Grand Master, the Prince of Wales (later King Edward VII) took part in Grand Lodge processions in the Provinces, including the laying of the two foundation stones of Truro Cathedral.

The Diamond Jubilee of Queen Victoria was celebrated in Welshpool in 1897 with a procession that included 'the Welshpool Lodge of Free Masons, No. 998, led by the Lodge Tyler John Whittall' – with drawn sword.

In 1929 the Pro Grand Master, Lord Ampthill, accompanied by Grand Officers in full regalia, laid the foundation stone of the new Shakespeare Memorial Theatre in Stratford-upon-Avon.

Although it is rare these days, given that in the past Freemasons have publicly paraded around towns in their regalia, it is still difficult to argue that Freemasonry is some form of secret society.

Regalia

In addition to aprons and gloves, there are other pieces of regalia such as medals that are also regularly worn by Masons. These are known in Masonic circles as jewels. The jewels are usually issued to celebrate some form of Masonic anniversary. For example, once a Master has completed his year in the Chair he is usually awarded a Past Master's breast jewel to wear in perpetuity. The form of the jewel varies but

The logo of Pioneer Lodge No. 9065 which makes it quite clear that the membership of the Lodge is closely linked with the Scouting Movement.

usually incorporates the lodge logo or motif. Jewels may also be struck to celebrate the Founding of a lodge and, at the other end of the scale, to commemorate the centenary or even bicentenary of a lodge. Some of the jewels are pieces of exquisite workmanship and until the Second World War were often made of solid gold.

Rolled Up Trouser leg?

A Candidate when he enters the Lodge Room for the first time is specially attired for the occasion. Shirt unbuttoned to expose his left-breast, left trouser leg rolled up and wearing a slipper on his right foot. Any metallic substances such as coins and indeed cufflinks and watches are left behind in the Preparation Room until after the ceremony.

Almost everything to do with Masonic ritual is symbolic. Thus the Candidate enters the room metaphorically poor and penniless. His right foot is slipshod: in middle-eastern culture the removal of a shoe is an accepted method of entering into a solemn and legal agreement. The Candidate has to declare in the ceremony that he is a 'free man'. Slaves would be required to wear an ankle chain that would leave a permanent scar – exposing the left leg demonstrates the lack of any such scar.

To Freemasons the practice serves several different purposes: to the Candidate it represents a situation that he is never likely to forget. It serves to remind him that he arrives at the door poor and penniless and he is made to feel suitably humble.

As far as the other members of the lodge are concerned, it reminds them of their own Initiation and is also an important part of the bonding process. In so far as the ridicule is concerned, the Masonic Initiation ceremony is no different in style and content to many other Initiation Ceremonies found in the world outside Freemasonry, such as the completion of apprenticeships, students, trade unions and other fraternal societies.

Royalty and Freemasonry

The connection between Royalty and Freemasonry goes back some 275 years when HRH Frederick Lewis (1707-1751), the eldest son of George II, was initiated in 1737. Three brothers of George III – Edward, Duke of York (1739-1767), William, Duke of Gloucester (1743-1805) and Henry, Duke of Cumberland (1721-1765) – were all members of the Craft.

George IV (1762-1830), the eldest son of George III, was Grand Master from 1790 until 1813 when he accepted the role of Grand Patron of the Order.

King William IV (1765-1837), who succeeded his brother George IV, was initiated in 1786 and was elected Past Grand Master of the 'Moderns' in 1787. His brothers – Frederick, Duke of York (1763-1827) and Ernest, Duke of Cumberland (1771-1851) – were both keen Freemasons whilst Edward, Duke of Kent (1767-

1820) and Augustus, Duke of Sussex (1773-1843) served as Grand Masters of the Antients and Moderns respectively. The Duke of Sussex became the first Grand Master of the United Grand Lodge of England in 1813.

Following the death of the Duke of Sussex there was a gap in royal participation in the Craft, for no other reason than that there were no Princes of the Blood Royal eligible to join.

This lapse was remedied when Edward VII (1841-1910), the eldest son of Queen Victoria, was initiated in Sweden in 1868. A most enthusiastic Mason and very supportive of Freemasonry, he was Grand Master in this country from 1874 until his accession in 1901, when he became Protector of the Craft. He also found time to be First Grand Principal of the Royal Arch, Grand Master of the Mark, Grand Master of the Knights Templar and Grand Patron of the Ancient and Accepted Rite.

HRH Albert, Duke of York (later King George VI) in his regalia as Provincial Grand Master for Middlesex – 1924 to 1936.

Arthur, Duke of Connaught (1850-1942), the third son of Queen Victoria, was as enthusiastic a Freemason as his elder brother, whom he succeeded as Grand Master from 1901 to 1939. He also held the offices of Provincial Grand Master for Sussex, District Grand Master Bombay, First Grand Principal of the Royal Arch, Grand Master of the Mark, Grand Master of Knights Templar and Grand Patron of the Ancient and Accepted Rite.

Although George V was not a Freemason, his two sons – who respectively became King Edward VIII (1894-1972) and King George VI (1895-1952) – were very active Freemasons.

Edward VIII whilst Prince of Wales was initiated in 1919 and was Provincial Grand Master of Surrey from 1924 to 1936.

In recent times the most enthusiastic of Royal Freemasons has undoubtedly been Albert, Duke of York who succeeded his brother Edward VIII on his abdication in 1936 as King George VI.

In response to his toast at the dinner following his Initiation the Duke of York is reported as saying:

> *I have always wished to become a Freemason, but owing to the war I have had no opportunity before this of joining the Craft. All my life I have heard of Freemasonry, and though there has always been a certain mystery attached to it, I have learned that Freemasons in this country have been a great help to the poor and friendless, and have been notable for their efforts on behalf of children. One can see, by the great Masonic Institutions and schools, how successful their work has been in this cause, and I like to think that in the future I shall be associated in their great work.*

In 1924 the Duke of York was installed as Provincial Grand Master of Middlesex. A Prince of the Blood Royal, with all his other duties and responsibilities, might be expected to attend the annual meeting as Provincial Grand Master but little else. The Duke however relished the role and took an active part in the work of the Province, including becoming in 1931 the Provincial Grand Master for Middlesex in the Mark.

He later acknowledged that his tenure as Provincial Grand Master helped him overcome his stammer and he attributed the improvement '...to the ritual and ceremonies I was obliged to conduct as a Freemason and Provincial Grand Master.'

In 1936 the Grand Lodge of Scotland was due to celebrate its bicentenary and the Prince of Wales had accepted the office of Grand Master Mason of Scotland. However, King George V died in January 1936 and on becoming Edward VIII, as protocol demanded, he resigned all his various Masonic offices. Accordingly the Duke of York was approached to take on the role – but there was a problem: to be Grand Master Mason of Scotland one had to be a member of a Scottish lodge. It says everything about the man that, rather than chose an 'upmarket' lodge in Edinburgh, he instead joined Glamis Lodge No. 99, a small village Lodge, the Master of which was a postman.

The Duke's rule as Grand Master Mason did not last long: he was installed on 30 November 1936 and King Edward VIII abdicated on 11 December 1936, so leading to the Duke's resignation.

In the ordinary course of events, on acceding to the throne the previous protocol was for the King not to take any further active participation in Freemasonry but become Patron the Craft, as in the case of George IV and Protector of Craft with Edward VII. However, George VI wished to continue his active association with Freemasonry and at an 'especial' meeting of Grand Lodge held to celebrate the

Coronation at the Albert Hall on 30 June 1937 he was installed as Past Grand Master. His address to the Brethren assembled on that occasion clearly demonstrates his feelings in respect of Freemasonry and what it meant to him:

> *...I have, since my initiation in 1919, been greatly interested in my association with Freemasonry. My work as a Provincial Grand Master for over thirteen years and in other directions gave me real pleasure, and I was sorry when it became necessary for me to cease my activities. In this work the Queen also, to whose family connection with the Craft you have alluded, has been interested, and has attended with me various gatherings – for instance the great Festival of the Royal Masonic Benevolent Institution in 1931. Today the pinnacle of my Masonic life has been reached by my investiture at your hands...with the insignia of Past Grand Master, an honour for which I thank you, and which is greatly appreciated...*

As far as his Royal duties allowed, the King continued to be actively involved as a Freemason until shortly before his untimely death and this included the Installation of three successive Grand Masters.

The first Installation was that of his younger brother, George, Duke of Kent (1902-1942) – the fourth son of George V and the father of the present Duke of Kent. The Duke of Kent succeeded his great-uncle, the Duke of Connaught, as Grand Master and was installed by the King in his capacity as Past Grand Master at a ceremony at Olympia on 19 July 1939, witnessed by some 12,000 Freemasons.

Tragically the Duke of Kent's rule was cut short when he was killed in an air crash in 1942 whilst serving in the RAF.

On 1 June 1943 George VI as Past Grand Master installed the Earl of Harewood as Grand Master at a ceremony at Freemasons' Hall. Unfortunately, the Earl died suddenly in 1947 – this meant that, for the third time since acceding to the throne, on 23 March

Issued as part of the '1946 Victory Issue,' the 3d Victory Stamp is filled with Masonic symbolism; the design was chosen by King George VI, a keen and enthusiastic Freemason.

1948 at an 'especial' Grand Lodge held at the Albert Hall the Past Grand Master King George installed the Duke of Devonshire as Grand Master. It was the last time that the King officiated at a Masonic ceremony, but is a clear indication of the seriousness with which he undertook his obligations as a Freemason. Following the death of the Duke of Devonshire in 1950, the King was due to install the Earl of Scarborough as Grand Master on 6 November 1951, but ill health prevented him from doing so and sadly he himself died on 2 February 1952 at the tragically young age of 56.

The following piece of ritual, taken from the Charge to the Initiate, could have been written with George VI very much in mind:

> *...in every age Monarchs themselves have been promoters of the Art, have not thought it derogatory to their dignity to exchange the Sceptre for the Trowel, have patronised our mysteries and joined in our assemblies.*

Freemasonry continues to receive Royal support – Prince Philip, Duke of Edinburgh was initiated in Navy Lodge No. 2612 in 1952 and remains a subscribing member; and the Kent branch of the Royal Family is still very much involved in the organisation of Freemasonry in this country. Edward, Duke of Kent was initiated in 1963 and elected as Grand Master for the first time in 1967 when Grand Lodge celebrated its 275th anniversary. In 2017 we look forward, *Deo volente*, to his presiding at the tercentenary celebrations of Grand Lodge and his 50th anniversary as Grand Master. The Duke of Kent's younger brother, Prince Michael of Kent, was initiated in 1974 and has been Provincial Grand Master of Middlesex and Grand Master of the Grand Lodge of Mark Master Masons since 1982.

After 275 years of Royal support for Freemasonry, long may the connection continue.

Secret Handshakes

The grip or token of recognition is 'the secret handshake' of the title of the book. This token or handshake should enable one Mason to recognise another by day as well as by night.

Whilst a limp handshake is usually a sure indication that the person concerned is not a Freemason, a firm handshake is no certainty that he is.

Each of the Three Degrees requires pressure to be applied to a different part of the other's hand. During the course of a lodge meeting great care is taken to ensure that the thumb is placed in exactly the right position. Out of the Lodge Room it is not easy to reproduce this with any degree of certainty; hence it is extremely unlikely that a Freemason would recognise a fellow Freemason simply by means of a handshake!

I am sorry if this comes as a great disappointment to readers, but, as often in life, the reality does not measure up to the expectation.

Secret Society or a Society with secrets

The detractors of Freemasonry maintain that it is a Secret Society. The pat answer on the part of Freemasons, in the past, has been to retort that it is not a Secret Society but a Society with Secrets. That is, of course, perfectly true. However the nuance on the part of the detractors is that it is the membership that is secret. One does not know who is and who is not a Freemason. Hence their rationale for calls that application forms for certain types of employment or public office should carry a declaration as to membership of the Freemasons – or rather membership of secret societies, for example, the Freemasons. This fallacy fails to recognise the essential difference between secrecy and privacy. There is nothing secret about membership. Freemasons in this country do not advertise their membership – for the very good reason that they should not be seen to be touting for business or attempting to gain some commercial advantage as a direct result of their membership. Details of members are to be found, for example, in Masonic Yearbooks and each lodge will have a membership list that is circulated to all its members. Masonic meeting places are clearly advertised and listed in periodicals such as *Yellow Pages* and are easily found with location maps through media such as Google. So far, no secrecy. Most towns and cities will have a golf club in the vicinity and the majority of the members will be drawn from the locale. Try phoning to get a list of members or the contact details of an individual member, and you will not be surprised to be given short shrift, either on the straightforward grounds of privacy or even the Data Protection Act! Why should Freemasonry be any different?

Self-help

Much is made of the fact that Freemasons always look after their own – which is absolutely true, but not the whole story. At the time when Freemasonry was formally established in this country, 1717, there was no unemployment benefit, no national insurance scheme to provide pensions, no national health service and no one to bury you if you could not afford it. A number of organisations have been set up over the years to provide such services and a financial safety net to their members. Examples include City Guilds and London Livery Companies, Trade Unions, Oddfellows and the like.

All the various state benefits have developed and increased, to the extent that today self-help on the part of fraternal societies has diminished proportionally. The different Masonic Charities and the benefits they provide for Freemasons are detailed separately, but it is true to say that they kick-in as far as Freemasons are concerned when all other avenues have been exhausted. The criteria used to determine the level of financial assistance that should be given mirrors the criteria that are used for state aid.

The fact that most Masons are now not dependent on Masonic charity for financial assistance means that all of the Charities concerned are able to make substantial donations to non-Masonic charities working in the same areas for the benefit of the community at large.

The purpose of this book is not to extol the virtues of Freemasonry as such and information about the range of work being done is easily found through the Internet. Suffice it to say that you would be very surprised at both the range and size of the grants being made. It certainly will not be found in any of the national newspapers, but more often than not may be found in the local press. I recall a grant of £3.1 million being made to the National Osteoporosis Society in 2006 to celebrate the sesquicentenary of a Masonic organisation – absolutely no mention in any of the national media, despite it being the largest grant ever received by the Society.

Spectrum of Freemasonry

One of the characteristics of Freemasonry is the range of opportunities it potentially offers to its members, in terms of what they are able to gain from it in a personal sense. At the two extremes of the spectrum are the esoteric wing at the one end and what I term the knife-and-fork Masons at the other.

The knife-and-fork Masons are easy to describe – they go to lodge meetings on a regular basis, four or five times a year, sit through the ritual and afterwards enjoy a good meal and a good drink, together with the fellowship and camaraderie that Freemasonry has to offer. From my perspective there is absolutely nothing wrong with that whatsoever. Freemasonry is after all both a hobby and a leisure activity to be enjoyed. At the other end of the spectrum is the very serious Mason, who also no doubt enjoys the social aspects of Freemasonry, but to him the most important element is the ritual, or rather the meaning or the spirituality perceived to be contained within the ritual. Thus the Three Degrees of Craft Masonry – Entered Apprentice, Fellow Craft and Master Mason – may at their most basic level be seen in terms of birth, development as a man and contemplation of inevitable death.

Between the two extremes are the vast majority of Freemasons who recognise the basic lessons lying behind the symbolism of the ritual but are not inclined to analyse it further.

Symbolism of Freemasonry

Most members of the public are familiar with the Square and Compasses as the iconic symbol of Freemasonry. It is, for example, to be found on many Masonic buildings in this country and overseas. Almost everything to do with Freemasonry and Masonic ritual is surrounded with symbolism. Indeed, Freemasonry can be defined as a 'system of morality, veiled in allegory and illustrated by symbols'. There are more than eighty different examples of Masonic symbolism that can be found within the ritual. To give a flavour, the following is taken from the explanation of the Working Tools in the First Degree:

> *...they are the 24-inch Gauge, the common Gavel, and Chisel. The 24-inch Gauge is to measure our work, the common Gavel to knock off all superfluous knobs and excrescences, and the Chisel to further smooth and prepare the stone and render it fit for the hands of the more expert workman. But, as we are not all operative Masons, but rather free and accepted or speculative, we apply these tools to our morals. In this sense, the 24-in Gauge represents the twenty-four hours of the day, part to be spent in prayer to Almighty God, part in labour and refreshment, and part in serving a friend or Brother in time of need, without detriment to ourselves or connections. The common Gavel represents the force of conscience, which should keep down all vain and unbecoming thoughts which might obtrude during any of the aforementioned periods, so that our words and actions may ascend unpolluted to the Throne of Grace. The Chisel points out to us the advantages of education, by which means alone we are rendered fit members of regularly organised Society.*

The three Craft Degrees are based on events relating to the building of King Solomon's Temple in Jerusalem and many of the incidents and characters represented may be found in the Bible, from which the original writers of the ritual undoubtedly took their inspiration.

Trade Unions

The association between Trade Unions and Freemasonry is not a subject that readily springs to mind and indeed has been sadly neglected by Masonic scholars. Professor Andrew Prescott has highlighted two pieces of interest. One is an article that appeared in *The Freemason* in 1925 by B. Springett and the other is by Andy Durr in 1987 in *Ars Quatuor Coronatorum* (the annual transactions of the Quatuor Coronati Lodge No. 2076, the premier Lodge of Masonic research in England) entitled 'Ritual of Association and Organisations of the Common People'. The latter article emphasises the link between the use of ritual in Unions and the practices of Friendly Societies such as the Oddfellows, Ancient Order of Druids and the Free Gardeners. The author also points out that the boilermakers and blacksmiths were still using ritual Initiation at the beginning of the twentieth century, and notes that in 1963, when the boilermakers, blacksmiths and shipwrights formed a new union, they issued a new ritual book, which was still in use in 1987. This merely reinforces the fact that the use of ritual Initiation is not by any means restricted to Freemasonry.

Travelling Military Lodges
Travelling Military Lodges greatly helped in the early expansion of lodges overseas. The four home Grand Lodges of England – the Moderns* (1717), Ireland (1725), Scotland (1736) and England – the Antients* (1751) all issued travelling Warrants to regiments of the British Army. The first to do so was the Grand Lodge of Ireland as early as 1731. Whereas normally a Grand Lodge would grant a Warrant to enable a lodge to be held in a particular town or locality, the Warrant granted to a regiment enabled it to hold meetings wherever the regiment happened to be stationed. The primary purpose of the Warrant was to allow the Initiation of members of the regiment; however it also allowed for the Initiation of local civilians if 'no other Lodge was available'. This was very often the case and it meant that when the regiment eventually moved off, the civilians that remained behind took over and were granted a Warrant to hold a lodge permanently in their own right. Military Lodges contributed particularly to the spread of Freemasonry in America and India. It is estimated that some 500 lodges were formed worldwide in this way. The only remaining Travelling Warrant in existence today is that of Lodge Glittering Star No. 322, originally granted to the 29th Regiment of Foot (now known as the Worcestershire and Sherwood Foresters Regiment) by the Grand Lodge of Ireland in 1759. As a Travelling Lodge it does not have a home base as such but continues to meet in various locations in the United Kingdom as the guest of local lodges.

> *The Antients and the Moderns became the United Grand Lodge of England in 1813.*

William Morgan Affair and the Anti-Masonry Party
One of the criticisms of Freemasonry relates to the various Obligations taken by Freemasons and the dire things that will happen to them if they ever divulge the secrets of Freemasonry.

No one in this country has ever suffered any of the penalties as a result of making public the so-called secrets of Freemasonry.

Given the number of men that have become Masons in this country (let alone throughout the world) since the first recorded making of a Freemason in 1646, that is surprising, especially given the general antipathy toward Freemasonry. The fact that no cases have come to light may well be a consequence of the fact that there *are* no such incidents to be brought forward!

There is however one infamous allegation from the USA, concerning a William Morgan, who was allegedly murdered by American Freemasons in 1826 for threatening to disclose the secrets of Freemasonry.

The case of Morgan is interesting both because of the consequences it had for American Freemasonry, and also politically with the formation of the first 'third party' in American politics – the Anti-Masonic Party, which formed part of the anti-Masonic movement. One cannot do justice to this subject in the short space available, given that it has resulted in a number of books and detailed research papers on what was a fascinating social phenomenon. The Bibliography and Reading List gives some suggestions for those interested in pursuing the subject.

The basic facts surrounding the story and the eventual outcome involve a William Morgan, who in today's parlance would be described in court as a man of 'bad character'. Although it cannot be established if he were ever made a Mason in a Craft lodge, there is evidence that he was involved with a Royal Arch Chapter in Batavia, a town in the north-west of New York State, towards the Canadian border and Niagara Falls. It would appear that, being in financial difficulty, he entered into some form of arrangement with a local printer to publish a book exposing the secrets of Freemasonry. He made details of his proposed project widely known – to the extent that the local Freemasons took grave exception to the possibility of this publication.

In September 1826 Morgan was arrested for theft and, although acquitted, was immediately rearrested for failure to pay a debt of $2.68 and jailed. His debt was paid by persons unknown and when he was released from jail he was met by several men who took him, apparently against his own will, by coach the 125-odd miles to Fort Niagara – and that is the last that anything was ever seen or heard of Morgan. Suffice it to say that there is no definitive proof that, if anything untoward happened to Morgan, it was at the hands of the Freemasons.

The affair did give rise to a substantial amount of ill feeling and downright antagonism towards Freemasonry. A number of politicians, notably Thurlow Weed, took advantage of the situation and used the incident as a means of discrediting Freemasonry in general by encouraging the usual claims that Freemasons looked after their own and ensured they obtained the best positions in their particular sphere of public life. The Morgan Affair was certainly a catalyst in the formation of the Anti-Masonry Party, which served a very useful purpose in providing a vehicle for general dissatisfaction on a number of different local issues at the time. In terms of being a shrewd and opportunist politician, almost the only thing that one needs to know about Thurlow Weed is that when a body was washed up in October 1827 (that looked nothing like Morgan) Thurlow's alleged comment was to the effect that it was 'a good enough Morgan' until after the election. As with many 'one-issue' parties, once the initial anti-Masonic fervour had diminished somewhat, the party broadened its base – to the extent that in 1832 it nominated as its presidential candidate a former Freemason, William Wirt, who gained nearly 8% of the popular vote.

The antagonism had a catastrophic effect on American Masonry. In 1827 there were 227 lodges in the Grand Lodge of New York. In 1835 the number had fallen to 41. In the State of Vermont, every single lodge surrendered its Warrant or became dormant. The situation was similar in Pennsylvania, Massachusetts, Connecticut and Rhode Island; with a similar, but lesser, knock-on effect in other States. It took a considerable period of time to make good the collateral damage arising from the Morgan Affair.

Women and Freemasonry

There are a number of instances, some apocryphal, of women being initiated into male Masonic lodges. This is usually as a consequence of the woman concerned somehow eavesdropping on a ceremony and on being discovered, then initiated into the lodge, thereby preserving the secrets of Freemasonry.

One of the more fanciful examples is depicted in an engraving by T. Wilkins of 1754 and described as follows:

> *The Chamber Maid, Moll, a Girl very fat,*
> *Lay hid in the Garret, as sly as a cat,*
> *To find out the Secret of Masons below,*
> *Which no one can tell, & themselves do not know.*

> *Moll happened to slip, & the Ceiling broke thro,*
> *And hung in the posture you have in your view,*
> *Which frightened the Masons, tho doing no Evil*
> *Who stoutly cried out, the Devil, the Devil.*

> *With Phiz white as Apron, the Masons ran down,*
> *And call'd up the Parson, his Clerk, & the Town,*
> *To lay the poor Devil thus pendant above:*
> *Who instead of Old Nick spy'd the Temple of Love.*

> *Come, all prying Lasses, take warning by Moll,*
> *The subject of this, the Print and the Droll,*
> *To get at a Secret which ne'er can be known,*
> *By an unlucky slip she discover'd her own.*

And the Masons may learn, without touching hoops,
That some of the Brothers are not Nicumpoops,
That Parson and Clerk, with their sanctified Faces
Had a peep at Moll's Rouser, & just so the Case is.

A more reliable example relates to Elizabeth St Leger, who was born in 1693. The only daughter of the first Viscount Doneraile, the Initiation was supposed to have taken place at his house. In the early days of Freemasonry it was quite usual for lodge meetings to take place in private houses. The Lodge was subsequently warranted in 1735 as No. 44 and was still meeting in 1791.

Adding to the credibility of the story is that Lady Elizabeth, who later married Richard Aldworth of Newmarket, County Cork in 1713 at the age of 20, became a patroness of the Craft, a position accepted by her contemporaries. Her name crops up in early Irish Masonic history and in the book written in 1744 by Dr

T. Wilkins' engraving of 1754, purporting to depict a lodge meeting in Canterbury
and interrupted by an eavesdropping lady (as described in rhyme above).

D'Assigny *A Serious and Impartial Enquiry*. Mrs Elizabeth Aldworth and her son Boyle Aldworth, together with a large number of Masons, were subscribers to the book. There is also a portrait of her hanging in the Masonic Hall in Cork, wearing a trowel pendant from her left shoulder and a Masonic apron trimmed with blue silk.

Women's Freemasonry

The proscription of women members contained in the *Constitutions* of English Freemasonry effectively excluded them from the movement as it swept through Europe and the colonial world in the early eighteenth century. France however was the outstanding exception, in that lodges with women members were established from the 1730s onwards and quickly became popular. Set up to win the loyalty and sympathy of women, to 'allow the fair sex to take part in charity and philosophy', their members were the wives or female relatives of Masons.

The meetings of these lodges stopped short of divulging anything of Masonic importance and their charming and light-weight rituals omitted key Masonic elements such as the Working Tools of the Degrees.

Some of the lodges became associated with specific male Masonic lodges and, because each lodge was under the 'protection' of a male Craft lodge and male officials from a regular lodge had to be present at their ceremonies, they became known as Lodges of Adoption. These increased in number until the Grand Orient of France – then the regulatory body for French Freemasonry – took control of the whole of *Maçonnerie d'Adoption* in 1774 and consolidated it as a specific Rite of four degrees. These were named Apprentice, Companion, Mistress and Perfect Mistress. Each female officer had a male counterpart, and ceremonies could not take place unless a male Mason was present. Nevertheless, membership was reserved for women only, even though men from the 'protector lodge' were obliged to attend. The ritual and symbolism became more serious: they were based on male Freemasonry and included elements from the Scriptures (particularly Genesis), such as Jacob's Ladder and the Tower of Babel. Most French cities and large towns had a Lodge of Adoption by 1780. Pre-Revolution, the lodges had an almost exclusively upper class membership – for example, the Princess de Lamballe, confidente of Marie Antoinette, presided over the *Contrat Social* Lodge; in 1775 the Duchess of Bourbon was installed as Grand Mistress of Adoptive Masonry. Some scholars maintain that, rather than regarding women in Lodges of Adoption as being offered an inferior role to make up for their exclusion from official Masonry, they were in fact able to pursue through the ritual of Freemasonry the Enlightenment principle of fraternity and carry this forward into the public sphere by their acts of charity.

During the Revolution male Freemasonry and the Adoptive Lodges were dormant. There was a short-lived resurgence during the First Empire under the patronage of the Empress Joséphine, wife of Napoléon I. This fashionable example resulted in a dramatic increase in the number of Adoptive Lodges. An incipient feminism developed, both in the way the women began to take charge of lodge proceedings and in the way that they concentrated their efforts on charity – in the public arena, charity became the face of Masonry and its disbursement reflected the power of organised women.

After the end of the First Empire, Adoptive Masonry declined in numbers and became less Masonic and more of a social event involving the whole family. The move towards the secularization of Masonry in the Lodges of Adoption prompted renewed calls for women to be admitted to the purer form of Freemasonry as practised by men and on the same terms as men. How this happened in France is described in the section on **Co-Masonry**.

As explained in that section mixed Freemasonry came to this country in 1902 when Annie Besant formed in London the Lodge of Human Duty No. 6 of the International Order of Co-Masonry, *Le Droit Humain*. By 1908 some members became dissatisfied with its theosophical and occult bias and they broke away to form another Order, the Honourable Fraternity of Antient Masonry (HFAM). This was headed by a man, the Revd Dr W.F. Cobb, and wanted to practise the three degrees of Craft Masonry on exactly the same lines as the United Grand Lodge of England (UGLE). The first three lodges founded in 1908 – Golden Rule No. 1, Emulation No. 2 and Lodge of Unity No. 3 – are still in existence. The Order originally consisted of both men and women, but the effect of the First World War and the sanctions of UGLE against participation by its members in mixed Masonry caused the number of male candidates to dwindle. After the refusal of UGLE to give Recognition to HFAM in 1921, it was decided to admit no more men. There were however a very few founder male members still in high office and it was not until the death of the last of these in 1935 that the Order officially became women-only. After Dr Cobb resigned in 1912, the Grand Master has always been a woman. In 1958 the name was changed to the *Order of Women Freemasons*, to make the gendered nature of the organisation quite clear. The OWF celebrated its Centenary at the Royal Albert Hall in 2008. The story of the Order can be read in *The Open Door: The History of the Order of Women Freemasons, 1908-2008*.

There is a second and smaller order for women in this country. In 1913 some members of HFAM tried to introduce the working of the Royal Arch Chapter in addition to the Craft, but they did so without consulting Grand Lodge and in a constitutionally irregular way. This move was rejected as precipitate and the group left to found their own Honourable Fraternity of Ancient Freemasonry (HFAF) in the same year. HFAF is still a flourishing organisation and celebrated its centenary meeting at Freemasons' Hall in 2013.

In England the relationship between the United Grand Lodge of England, or the 'Older Obedience' as it is known by women Freemasons, has been very cordial in recent years and the women increasingly use the men's Temples for meetings (and vice versa). In 1999 a statement was issued by UGLE for the advice of its members:

> There exist in England and Wales at least two Grand Lodges solely for women. Except that these bodies admit women, they are, so far as can be ascertained, otherwise regular in their practice. There is also one which admits both men and women to membership. They are not recognised by this Grand Lodge and inter-visitation may not take place. There are, however, discussions from time to time with the women's Grand Lodges on matters of mutual concern. Brethren are therefore free to explain to non-Masons, if asked, that Freemasonry is not confined to men.

Zion, The Protocols of the Learned Elders of

The *Protocols of the Learned Elders of Zion* were serialised in the *Morning Post* in July 1920 and subsequently published as a booklet – *The Jewish Peril* – later that year. The serialisation achieved considerable notoriety. The fact that *The Times* exposed *The Jewish Peril* as a hoax and a forgery in 1921 did little to allay the fears of those accused or prevent the widespread use of the document by those who saw advantage in exploiting an alleged Jewish/Masonic international conspiracy for world domination.

The following extracts from the total of twenty-four Protocols give a flavour of the whole distasteful document:

Protocol 4

1. Gentile masonry, blindly serves as a screen for us and our objects, but the plan of action of our force, even its very abiding place, remains for the whole people an unknown mystery...

Protocol 11

1. The *goyim* are a flock of sheep, and we are their wolves. And you know what happens when the wolves get hold of the flock? ... for what purpose then have we invented this whole policy and insinuated it into the minds of the goys without giving them any chance to examine its underlying meaning? For what indeed if not in order to obtain in a roundabout way what is for our scattered tribe unattainable by the direct road? It is this which has served as the basis for our organization

of <u>secret</u> masonry which is not known to, and aims which are not even so much as suspected by, these goy cattle, attracted by us into the 'show' army of masonic lodges in order to throw dust in the eyes of their fellows.

Protocol 15

2. We shall create and multiply free Masonic lodges in all the countries of the world, absorb into them all who may become or who are prominent in public activity, for in these lodges we shall find our principal intelligence office and means of influence. All these lodges we shall bring under one central administration, known to us alone and to all others absolutely unknown, which will be composed of our learned elders. The lodges will have their representatives who will serve to screen the above-mentioned administration of *masonry* and from whom will issue the watchword and programme. In these lodges we shall tie together the knot which binds together all revolutionary and liberal elements...

Although denounced as forgeries, Hitler and the Nazis in Germany continued to use the *Protocols* as one of the central core policies to justify the persecution of Jews and Freemasons.

Bibliography and Suggested Reading List

Barker-Cryer, N. *Masonic Halls of England – The Midlands* (1989).

Calderwood, P. *Freemasonry and the Press in the Twentieth Century* (2013).

Carr, H. *The Freemason at Work* (1977 ed.).

Carr, H. ed. *Early French Exposures 1737-1751* (1971).

Carr, H. *Harry Carr's World of Freemasonry* (1984).

Castells, F. de *The Genuine Secrets in Freemasonry prior to A.D. 1717* (1930).

Coil, H.W. *Coil's Masonic Encyclopedia* (1961).

Cooper, R.L.D. *The Red Triangle: A History of Anti-Masonry* (2011).

Dennis, V.S. *Discovering Friendly and Fraternal Societies: their badges and regalia* (2005).

Dewar, J. *The Unlocked Secret: Freemasonry Examined* (1966).

Dyer, C.F.W. *Symbolism in Craft Masonry* (1986 ed.)

Fajardo, R.S. *The Brethren – Masons in the struggle for Philippine Independence* (1998).

Gould, R.F. *The History of Freemasonry* (1870).

Halleran, M.A. *The Better Angels of Our Nature: Freemasonry in the American Civil War* (2010).

Hamill, J. *The Craft – a history of English Freemasonry* (1986).

Hamill, J. *History of English Freemasonry* (1994).

Harland-Jacobs, J. *Builders of Empire – Freemasonry and British Imperialism, 1717-1927* (2007).

Hodapp, C. *Freemasons for Dummies* (2005).

Inman, H.F. *Masonic Problems and Queries* (1933).

Jackson, A.C.F. *English Masonic Exposures 1760-1769* (1986).

Jackson, K.B. *Beyond the Craft* (4th ed. 1994, rep. 2002).

Jeffers, H.P. *Freemasons – A history and exploration of the world's oldest secret society* (2005).

Jones, B.E. *Freemasons' Guide and Companion* (1953 ed., rep.1956).

Knight, T.A. *The Strange Disappearance of William Morgan* (1932).

Knoop, D., Jones, G.P. and Hamer, D. *The Early Masonic Catechisms* (1975 ed.).

Knoop, D. and others *Early Masonic Pamphlets* (1978).

Knoop, D. and Jones, G.P. *Genesis of Freemasonry* (1947, 1978 ed.).

Lane, J. *Masonic Records 1717 – 1894* (1895, 2000 ed.).

Library and Museum of Freemasonry, *English Royal Freemasons* (2010).

McArthur, J.E. *The Lodge of Edinburgh (Mary's Chapel) No. 1 Quartercentenary of minutes: 1599 –1999* (1999).

Mackenzie, K. *Royal Masonic Cyclopaedia of history, rites, symbolism, and biography* (1877).

Mendoza, H. *Serendipity* (1995).

Millar, A. *Freemasonry: A History* (2005).

Muir, R.K. 'The Morgan affair & its effect on Freemasonry', *AQC* 105 (1992), pp. 217-234.

Pick, F.L. and Knight, G.N. *The Freemason's Pocket Reference Book* (revised by F. Smyth,1983).

Pick, F.L. and Knight, G.N. *The Freemason's Pocket History of Freemasonry* (revised by F. Smyth, 1983).

Pilcher-Dayton, A. *The Open Door: The History of the Order of Women Freemasons, 1908-2008* (2008).

Roberts, A.E. *House Undivided: The Story of Freemasonry and the Civil War* (1961).

Stewart, T. ed. *Freemasonry and religion: many faiths, one brotherhood* (2006).

Stevenson, D. *The Origins of Freemasonry* (1988).

Stevenson, D. *The First Freemasons* (1988).

Wade, J. *'Go and do thou likewise': English Masonic Processions from the 18th to 20th Centuries* (Prestonian Lecture 2009).

Webb, J. *Rudyard Kipling, Man, Poet, Mason* (1996).

Wells, R.A. *Freemasonry in London from 1785* (1984).

Wells, R.A. *The Rise and Development of Organised Freemasonry* (1986).